M000194584

# The Principles of Beautiful Web Design, 4th Edition

Copyright © 2020 SitePoint Pty. Ltd.

**Product Manager:** Simon Mackie
**Editor:** Ralph Mason
**Cover Designer:** Alex Walker

## Notice of Rights

All rights reserved. No part of this book may be reproduced, stored in a retrieval system or transmitted in any form or by any means, without the prior written permission of the publisher, except in the case of brief quotations embodied in critical articles or reviews.

## Notice of Liability

The author and publisher have made every effort to ensure the accuracy of the information herein. However, the information contained in this book is sold without warranty, either express or implied. Neither the authors and SitePoint Pty. Ltd., nor its dealers or distributors will be held liable for any damages to be caused either directly or indirectly by the instructions contained in this book, or by the software or hardware products described herein.

## Trademark Notice

Rather than indicating every occurrence of a trademarked name as such, this book uses the names only in an editorial fashion and to the benefit of the trademark owner with no intention of infringement of the trademark.

Published by SitePoint Pty. Ltd.
Level 1, 110 Johnston St,
Fitzroy VIC 3065
Australia
Web: www.sitepoint.com
Email: books@sitepoint.com
ISBN 978-1-925836-36-3 (print)
ISBN 978-1-925836-37-0 (ebook)

## About the Authors

**Jason Beaird** is a designer and front-end developer with over ten years of experience working on a wide range of award-winning web projects. With a background in graphic design and a passion for web standards, he's always looking for accessible ways to make the Web a more beautiful place. When he's not pushing pixels in Photoshop or tinkering with markup, Jason loves sharing his passion for the Web with others. He writes about his ideas, adventures, and random projects on his personal site, jasongraphix.com[1].

**James George** is a professional web designer from the United States, who is passionate about the field of design. He loves connecting with other designers and developers. James enjoys working closely with clients and businesses to create powerful, beautiful web design solutions. You can find him on https://twitter.com/creativebeacon/Twitter[2].

**Alex Walker** has directed SitePoint's design thinking for two decades through front-end design, 50+ book covers and over 200 articles. His dream is to one day use CSS and SVG to create cold fusion (the process, not the language). You can find him from time to time on Twitter[3].

# About SitePoint

SitePoint specializes in publishing fun, practical, and easy-to-understand content for web professionals. Visit http://www.sitepoint.com/ to access our blogs, books, newsletters, articles, and community forums. You'll find a stack of information on JavaScript, PHP, Ruby, mobile development, design, and more.

---

[1.] http://jasongraphix.com
[2.] https://twitter.com/creativebeacon/
[3.] https://twitter.com/alexmwalker/

# Table of Contents

**Preface** ........................................................................................................ xii

Who Should Read This Book? ........................................................... xiii

Conventions Used ................................................................................ xv

Supplementary Materials ................................................................... xvi

Chapter 1:     **Layout and Composition** ....................................... 1

The Design Process ............................................................................... 2

    Discovery ............................................................................................ 3

    Client Meetings Don't Have to Take Place in an Office ................... 4

    Exploration ......................................................................................... 5

    Implementation ................................................................................. 5

Defining Good Design ........................................................................... 6

    Users Are Pleased by the Design but Drawn to the Content ........ 7

    Users Can Move about Easily via Intuitive Navigation .................. 8

    Users Recognize Each Page as Belonging to the Site .................... 9

Web Page Anatomy ............................................................................. 10

    The Containing block ...................................................................... 11

    The Logo ........................................................................................... 11

    The Navigation ................................................................................ 12

    The Content ...................................................................................... 12

The Footer........................................................................................................12

Whitespace ....................................................................................................13

Grid Theory ........................................................................................................13

The Rule of Thirds........................................................................................16

CSS Frameworks ..............................................................................................18

Balance ...............................................................................................................21

Symmetrical Balance ..................................................................................21

Asymmetrical Balance................................................................................ 24

Unity ...................................................................................................................28

Proximity .......................................................................................................28

Repetition......................................................................................................30

Emphasis............................................................................................................31

Placement......................................................................................................32

Continuance..................................................................................................32

Isolation.........................................................................................................33

Contrast......................................................................................................... 34

Proportion ..................................................................................................... 35

Bread-and-butter Layouts ............................................................................38

Left-column Navigation ..............................................................................38

Right-column Navigation............................................................................ 40

Three-column Navigation ............................................................................41

Navigationless Magazine Style................................................................... 43

Bare-bones Minimalism ............................................................................. 44

Break the Mould Layouts.................................................. 45

Web Trends............................................................................ 47

Video Backgrounds ...................................................... 48

Masonry Layouts............................................................. 49

Parallax Scrolling........................................................... 50

Finding Inspiration ........................................................... 50

Using a Morgue File ......................................................... 51

Responsive Design............................................................ 52

Screen Resolutions .......................................................... 53

How Do @media Queries Work? ........................... 54

Responsive Web Design Principles............................. 54

Always Design for "Mobile First" ......................... 54

Don't Jam Elements into the Mobile View ....... 55

SVG Is Your BFF .............................................................. 56

Responsive Frameworks ................................................ 56

The Project: Trashmonger ............................................. 59

Assets.................................................................................... 59

Requirements.................................................................... 60

Sitemap.................................................................................... 61

Wireframes........................................................................ 62

Chapter 2:      **Color**........................................................66

The Psychology of Color ............................................... 67

Color Associations ............................................................... 67

Red ......................................................................................... 68

Orange ................................................................................... 68

Yellow..................................................................................... 69

Green ..................................................................................... 70

Blue ........................................................................................ 71

Purple..................................................................................... 72

White...................................................................................... 73

Black....................................................................................... 74

Color Temperature ...................................................................... 75

Chromatic Value ........................................................................... 76

Saturation .............................................................................. 76

Color Theory 101 .......................................................................... 77

Red, Yellow, and Blue, or CMYK.................................................. 80

The Scheme of Things ................................................................. 83

A Monochromatic Color Scheme........................................ 83

Monochromatic Color Scheme in the Real World........... 84

An Analogous Color Scheme................................................ 88

Analogous Color Scheme Examples .................................. 89

A Complementary Color Scheme ....................................... 91

Complementary Color Scheme Examples....................... 92

Common Complementary Pitfalls...................................... 96

Split-complementary, Triadic, and Tetradic.................... 98

Other Variants.........................................................................................101

Creating a Palette ...................................................................................102

Hexadecimal Notation ..................................................................102

Color Tools and Resources ......................................................................103

Paletton ............................................................................................104

Colormind..........................................................................................105

Adobe Color ....................................................................................105

COLOURlovers..................................................................................106

Colour Contrast Checker .............................................................107

The Application: Choosing a Color Palette.........................................108


Chapter 3:      **Texture** .......................................................................**112**

Point ...........................................................................................................113

Line .............................................................................................................115

Shape...........................................................................................................116

Designing in CSS.............................................................................122

Rotation and Angles.......................................................................123

Directing the Eye ............................................................................124

Putting It Into Practice....................................................................126

Volume and Depth ...................................................................................127

Perspective.......................................................................................128

Proportion .........................................................................................128

Light and Shadow ..........................................................................129

From 3D Renders to Flat design.................................................130

Flat Design.................................................................................131

Is UI Design Still a Flat Earth? .............................................. 132

Photoshop Filters .................................................................... 133

Pattern.............................................................................................. 133

Building Texture: Vintage, Patterned, Worn, and Nostalgic Styles ... 138

Paper Grain................................................................................ 138

Paints, Pencils and Other Traditional Media ......................141

Faded Memories ...................................................................... 142

The Digital Retro Look ........................................................... 143

Halftone and Ben Day Dots .................................................. 143

DIY Halftones............................................................................ 145

Starting Your Own Textural Trends ...................................... 147

Application: Adding a Design Motif Using SVG Patterns ...................... 147

Using a Pattern as a Motif.......................................................... 149

Chapter 4:     **Typography** ................................................... 151

Taking Type to the Web................................................................ 154

Self-hosted Web Fonts............................................................ 156

Web Font Services ................................................................... 157

Anatomy of a Letterform............................................................. 159

Text Spacing ................................................................................... 162

Horizontal Spacing.................................................................. 162

Vertical Spacing ...................................................................164

Text Alignment ..........................................................................165

Typeface Distinctions................................................................166

Serif Fonts .............................................................................167

Sans-serif Fonts....................................................................171

Handwritten Fonts .................................................................173

Fixed-width Fonts...................................................................176

Novelty Fonts ........................................................................178

Dingbat Fonts .......................................................................181

Finding Fonts..............................................................................183

Free Font Galleries................................................................184

Commercial Font Galleries ...................................................184

Individual Artists and Foundries...........................................185

Choosing the Right Fonts............................................................185

Establishing a Typographic System............................................188

Typical Body Font Sizes.......................................................189

Scaling Your Type .......................................................................189

Type Scaling in Practice .......................................................190

Mobile Considerations .........................................................191

Vertical Baseline Rhythm............................................................193

Vertical Baseline Rhythm Is a Tool, Not a Religion.......................198

The Takeaway .............................................................................199

The Project: Building a Type System............................................199

Creating a Basic Typography Style Guide................................201

Adding a Visual Grid.................................................................202

What Now?...................................................................................204


Chapter 5:    **Imagery** ..................................................**205**

What to Look For ........................................................................207

Question 1: Is It Relevant?....................................................207

Question 2: Is It Interesting? ...............................................208

Question 3: Is It Appealing? ...............................................209

Legitimate Image Sources .......................................................211

Take It or Make It.....................................................................211

Stock Photography .................................................................213

Getting Professional Help .....................................................224

How Not to Impress....................................................................227

Google Ganking........................................................................227

Hotlinking..................................................................................227

Clip Art......................................................................................228

Image Presentation....................................................................229

Creative Cropping ...................................................................229

Image Adjustments .................................................................235

Filters.........................................................................................241

File Formats and Resolutions..................................................246

Creative Image Treatments......................................................248

Using Images to Enhance Images........................................................249

Using Pure CSS to Enhance Images.................................................. 251

Breaking.........................................................................................254

The Project: Pulling the Design Together .......................................255

Pulling in the Pattern Motif ..............................................................258

Complete: Trashmonger v1.0 .............................................................. 260

Onward and Upward .............................................................................. 260

# Preface

When my wife and I moved into our house, one of our first major projects was to update the bathroom. The horribly gaudy floral wallpaper pattern, along with the gold sink fixtures, obnoxious mirrors, and tacky lighting, made us feel like we'd stepped into a previous decade every time we entered the master bathroom. Removing wallpaper is a tough job, but it's even more difficult when there are multiple layers of the stuff. This was the case with our bathroom. Apparently the previous homeowners' taste in wallpaper changed every few years, and rather than stripping off the wallpaper and starting over, they just covered ugly with more ugly. Ah, the joys of home ownership!

If there's one thing our renovation adventures have taught me, it's that there are strong parallels between designing a room's decor and designing a good website.

> *Good design is about the relationships between the elements involved, and creating a balance between them.*

Whether we're talking about a website or bathroom makeover, throwing up a new layer of wallpaper or changing the background color isn't a design solution in itself—it's just part of a solution. While we removed the wallpaper and rollered some paint onto our bathroom, we also had to change the light fixtures, remove the gold-trimmed shower doors, replace the mirrors, upgrade the lighting, paint the cabinets, change the switches and plugs, and scrape off the popcorn ceilings. If we'd just removed the tacky wallpaper and left all the other stuff, we'd still have an outdated bathroom. Website design is similar: you can only do so many minor updates before the time comes to scrap what you have and start over.

> *Fads come and go, but good design is timeless.*

Conforming to the latest design trends is a good way to ensure temporary public appeal, but how long will those trends last? As far as I know, there was hardly ever a time when marquee and blink tags were accepted as professional web design markup ... but scrolling JavaScript news tickers, "high readability" hit-counters, and chunky table borders have graced the home pages of many high-profile sites in the past. These are the shag carpets, sparkly acoustic ceilings, and faux wood paneling of the web design world. Take a trip in the Internet Wayback Machine, and look for late-nineties versions of some of the top Fortune 500 and pre-dot-com, boom-era websites. Try to find examples of good and bad design. In the midst of some of the most outdated, laughable websites, you're likely to find some pages that still look surprisingly relevant. Most likely, these designs aren't dependent on flashy Photoshop filters or trendy image treatments. As you read this book, keep in mind that good design transcends technology.

> *The finishing touches make a big impression.*

I've heard it argued that deep down, people really love "anti-marketing design." The idea is that we trust sites that have an unpolished appearance and feel amateurish. I think this argument misses the point. No matter what type of website you're developing, the design should be as intentional as the functionality. My wife and I didn't change the functionality of our bathroom with the work that we did. We just fine-tuned the details, but it made a world of difference. Some people might have been able to live with the bathroom the way it was, but I doubt you'd find anyone who would say it was exactly what they wanted.

Similarly, if you're spending time developing a website, you should take time to design it. Under no circumstances should the design feel unpolished or haphazard. If you want to come off as edgy, anti-marketing, and non-corporate, then do it, and do it well—but there's no reason to be ignorant about, or feel intimidated by, design.

Our goal with this book is simple: to present what we know about designing for the Web in a way that anyone can understand and apply. Why? Because the basics of website design should be common knowledge. We all live in and work on an internet that has been blindly covering up ugly with more ugly since its inception. It's time to break that chain and make bold moves toward better design.

– Jason

## Who Should Read This Book?

If you're squeamish about choosing colors, feel uninspired by a blank browser window, or get lost trying to choose the right font, this book is for you. I take a methodical approach to presenting traditional graphic design theory as it applies to today's website development industry. While the content is directed towards web programmers and developers, it provides a design primer and relevant examples that will benefit readers at any level.

xiv     The Principles of Beautiful Web Design, 4th Edition

## What's in This Book

This book comprises the following five chapters. You can read them from beginning to end to gain a complete understanding of the subject, or skip around if you only need a refresher on a particular topic.

### Chapter 1: Layout and Composition

An awareness of design relies heavily on understanding the spatial relationships that exist between the individual components of a design. The layout chapter kicks off the design process by investigating possible page components. With these blocks defined, we discuss some tools and examples that will help you start your own designs on a solid foundation. To wrap up this discussion, we'll begin a project that we'll follow through each chapter—Trashmonger.

### Chapter 2: Color

Perhaps the most mysterious aspect of design is the topic of color selection. Chapter 2 sheds light on this as we delve into both the aesthetic and scientific aspects of color theory. Armed with these simple guidelines, and some tips for creating harmonious color combinations, you'll see how anyone can choose a set of colors that work well together to complement the overall message of a website. Finally, we'll look at how our color palette influences our Trashmonger project.

### Chapter 3: Texture

An aspect of web design that's often overlooked, texture is the key to creating designs that stand out. By understanding how the individual elements of texture function, you'll learn how to use points, lines, and shapes to communicate and support your site's message on a number of levels. We'll then get to see firsthand how subtle textures helped shape the identity and character of our example website.

### Chapter 4: Typography

The importance of typography is undeniable. Type is everywhere, and understanding the mechanics of written language is essential for any visual designer. In this chapter, we'll dive beneath the surface of this rich topic, exploring the basics of the letterform, and investigating various typeface distinctions. We'll also construct a practical type system for our Trahmonger project.

### Chapter 5: Imagery

The necessary companions to any well-designed site are the images and illustrations that grace its pages. In the final chapter, we'll discuss what we should look for in the visual elements that we use on our pages, and locate sources of legitimate supporting imagery. Of course, finding the right image is often just the beginning. We'll also learn some image-editing basics before we see the final steps in our example project.

## Conventions Used

You'll notice that we've used certain typographic and layout styles throughout this book to signify different types of information. Look out for the following items.

### Code Samples

Code in this book is displayed using a fixed-width font, like so:

```
<h1>A Perfect Summer's Day</h1>
<p>It was a lovely day for a walk in the park.
The birds were singing and the kids were all back at school.</p>
```

Where existing code is required for context, rather than repeat all of it, ⋮ will be displayed:

```
function animate() {
    ⋮
new_variable = "Hello";
}
```

Some lines of code should be entered on one line, but we've had to wrap them because of page constraints. An ↪ indicates a line break that exists for formatting purposes only, and should be ignored:

```
URL.open("http://www.sitepoint.com/responsive-web-
↪design-real-user-testing/?responsive1");
```

## Tips, Notes, and Warnings

### Hey, You!

Tips provide helpful little pointers.

### Ahem, Excuse Me ...

Notes are useful asides that are related—but not critical—to the topic at hand. Think of them as extra tidbits of information.

### Make Sure You Always ...

... pay attention to these important points.

### Watch Out!

Warnings highlight any gotchas that are likely to trip you up along the way.

### CodePen Demo

This example has an associated CodePen demo

## Supplementary Materials

- https://www.sitepoint.com/community/ are SitePoint's forums, for help on any tricky problems.
- **books@sitepoint.com** is our email address, should you need to contact us to report a problem, or for any other reason.

# Layout and Composition

Chapter

**1**

For many web developers, myself included, the most intimidating part of the design process is getting started. Imagine for a moment that you're sitting at your desk with nothing other than a cup of coffee and the business card of a potential client who needs a basic corporate website. Usually, a business card speaks volumes about a company's identity, and can be used as design inspiration.

Unfortunately, that's not the case with the card for Smith's Services below. It's black and white, all text, no character. Bleurgh! Talk about a blank canvas! So, where do you go from here? You need a plan ... and you need to contact Mr. Smith. With some critical input from the client about what his company actually does, and by gathering information about the content you have to work with, you'll be able to come up with a successful design.

## SMITH'S SERVICES

**Jim Smith**
*Professional Service Associate*

100 Random Street
Suite 16
Somewhere, VA 54321

Tel. 867-5309
Fax. 555-2368

1-1. A bland client business card

Anyone, no matter what level of artistic talent, can come up with a design that works well and looks good. All it takes is a little experience and a working knowledge of some basic layout principles. So let's start with the basics, and before long you'll have the foundation necessary to design gallery-quality websites.

## The Design Process

Designing a website can be a double-edged sword. The process falls somewhere between art, science, and problem solving. Yes, we want to create an individual site that's aesthetically pleasing, but our highest priority should be to meet the needs of our client. These needs may be lofty and elaborate, or they may just be about making information available. If we fail to listen carefully, though, the entire project will come falling down. The process of creating a design comp, however, can be boiled down to just three key tasks: discovery, exploration, and implementation.

 **What's a Comp?**

The word **comp** is an abbreviation of the phrase "comprehensive dummy"—a term that comes from the print design world. It's a complete simulation of a printed layout that's created before the layout goes to press. In translating this term to web design, a comp is an image of a layout that's created before we begin to prototype the design in HTML.

## Discovery

The discovery component of the design process is about meeting the clients and learning what they do. This may feel a little counterintuitive, but gathering information about who your clients are and how they run their business is vital in coming up with an appropriate and effective design.

Before you schedule your first meeting with a client, spend some time researching their business. If they've asked you to design a website, they may currently be without one, but google them anyway. If you're unable to find any information about their business specifically, try to learn as much as you can about their industry before the first meeting. Whenever possible, the first meeting with a client should be conducted in person. Sometimes, distance will dictate that the meeting has to occur over the phone, but if the client is in town, schedule a time to meet face to face.

Keep in mind that this meeting is less about impressing the client, selling yourself, or selling a website than it is about communication and establishing just what it is the client wants. Try to listen more than you speak, and bring a pad for taking notes. If you bring a laptop or tablet with you to talk about website examples, limit the time spent using it. Computers have screens, and people tend to stare at them, which isn't conducive to a good meeting or to note taking. If you must drag some technology into the meeting, use a voice recording app to record the conversation—with the client's permission, of course. In my experience, though, pen and pad are less threatening and far less distracting to the often not-so-tech-savvy client.

## Client Meetings Don't Have to Take Place in an Office

Even when I worked for a company in a big office, I had some of my most productive client meetings at a café or over lunch. The feasibility of this approach depends on the client. If your contact seems to be more the formal business type, don't suggest it. In many cases, though, it's a good way to make a business meeting more personal.

Below are some of the questions I like to ask in initial client meetings, even if I've already established the answer myself via a search engine.

**If the project is a new website development:**

- What does the company do?
- What is your role in the company? (This question is especially important if this person is going to be your main point of contact.)
- Does the company have an existing logo or brand?
- What is your goal in developing a website?
- What information do you wish to provide online?
- Who are your competitors and do they have websites?
- Do you have examples of websites you like or dislike?

**If the project is to redesign an existing website, I also like to ask:**

- What are your visitors usually looking for when they come to your site?
- What are the problems with your current design?
- What do you hope to achieve with a redesign?
- Are there any elements of the current site that you want to keep?
- How do you think your visitors will react to a new site design?

**If the project is a new app development:**

- What is the goal of the app?
- What platforms does it need to work on (web/native)?

**In all three cases I like to ask:**

- Do you have examples of apps/sites you like or dislike?
- Are there competitors to the app/site in this field?
- Who comprises your target audience? Do its members share any common demographics, like age, sex, or a physical location?
- What kind of timeline do you have for the project and what is the budget?

Sometimes I start off with more questions than those listed here. Use your imagination and try to come up with some creative queries that will really give you more insight into the client's organization. If you're a programmer, avoid tech jargon. If you're a designer, avoid talking specifically about design. Sure, that may be all you're thinking about, but things like semantic markup and responsive layouts will likely mean very little to the client. Worse still, these types of conversations can bring misguided design opinions your way before you have a chance to start thinking about the design yourself.

## Exploration

The next stage of the design process is to take the information you've learned from the client back to your laboratory for analysis, dissection, and experimentation. You want to develop a firm grasp on all the information, products, and services they have to offer, and play around with how these could be arranged. Put yourself in the shoes of the website visitors and ask yourself what these people are looking for. If you're thinking about buying a product, what do you need to know before you buy? If you're signing up for a service, where would you learn about the different offerings and which level of service you need? What is the clearest title possible for page X, and how many steps does it take to reach page Y?

In the world of web design, this is the beginning of a process known as **information architecture**, or IA for short. For expansive websites and complex web applications, information architecture is a career in itself, but the guiding principles of this field can provide a solid foundation for even the smallest websites. For the exploration stage of our process, we want to focus on organizing the content and flow of the website into a structure we can design around.

Two of the most essential tools for this task are scrap paper (or a whiteboard if you have one) and a big block of sticky notes. Make a list of all the bits and pieces of the website and start arranging them into groups and subgroups. These are likely to move around quite a bit, and that's where the sticky notes come in handy. If you make a note for every section, subsection, and page of the site, you can arrange them on a wall in the order they'll appear in your site's navigation. You'll want to avoid overwhelming the visitors with too many options, but you also don't want to bury information too deeply within the site—that is, too many clicks away from the home page. There are no hard and fast rules for this activity; just make the information as obvious and as easy to reach as possible.

## Implementation

Now that we've thought through how we want to organize the information we're working with, the implementation step of our design process begins with creating a layout. Regardless of the project, try to avoid being caught up in the technology associated with building websites—at least at first. At this point, it's unimportant whether the site is going to comprise straight HTML, a template for a content management system, or a Ruby on Rails application. The bottom line is that we have an interface to design and a blank sheet of paper. "Paper?" That's right, paper. Did you really think I was going to let you go back to your precious computer already? No way. Here's why: it's easy to lose focus on the design if you start thinking about the layout in front of a computer. If you start out on paper, you can ignore the technical limitations of browsers and CSS, and focus on how you want the final product to look. You might think that all good designers carry around fancy, hard-bound sketch books in which they flourish expensive markers and paintbrushes to design Da Vinci-esque renderings of potential web page layouts. For my part, I use a 79-cent, spiral-bound notebook and any writing instrument I can find on my desk that still works.

I start out by sketching a few possible layouts. After I've produced a few, I decide on one I like, jump into Photoshop, and use the rectangle tool to block out the areas I've marked down on paper. Once I've defined my layout, I experiment with foreground and background colors until I have a solid color scheme. I continue twiddling the Photoshop knobs and pushing around pixels until, finally, magically, I have a comp to show the client.

Simple, right? Okay, perhaps I skipped a few steps in that brief description. Honestly, though, when people ask me how I do what I do, they usually receive a similar explanation. The truth is that there are reams of now-subconscious information from my past experience and those old college design and art classes that have helped me to define my own design process.

Learning how to design is like learning how to program. Some people have a bit of a knack for it, but anyone can learn. Just as there's good code and ugly code, there's good design and ugly design. Learning some of the principles and conventions associated with design will help you to understand the difference between the good, the bad, and the ugly, moving you towards establishing your own design process.

## Defining Good Design

There are two main standpoints from which most people determine whether a website design is "good" or "bad". There's a strict usability angle, which focuses on functionality, the effective presentation of information, and efficiency. Then there's the purely aesthetic perspective, which is all about the artistic value and visual appeal of the design. Some people become caught up in the aesthetics and graphics, and forget about the user, while some usability gurus get lost in their user testing and forget about visual appeal. In order to reach people and retain their interest, it's essential to maximize both.

The most important point to keep in mind is that design is about communication. If you create a website that works and presents information well, but looks ugly or fails to fit with the client's brand, no one will want to use it. Similarly, if you make a beautiful website that's hard to use or inaccessible, people will leave. Indeed, the elements and functionality of a finished website design should work as a single cohesive unit. Below are listed some of the reasons for this.

## Users Are Pleased by the Design but Drawn to the Content

One of the biggest concerns among usability professionals is the time it takes users to scan the page for the information they want, be it a piece of content, a link to another page, or a form field. The design should not be a hindrance; it should act as a conduit between the user and the information.

1-2. Tall, True and Tangled — travellers' tales

Tall, True and Tangled[1], above, is a video travel journal following the journey of two friends through Newfoundland and Labrador in Canada. The "*tall, true and tangled*" in the title refers to the stories that Marlee and Mirella collect along the way. This idea of striking out on a grand adventure has been cleverly captured in the design, where the bird's-eye, map view of a beautiful Labrador cove perfectly frames a calligraphic logo. This logo then tails off to become a meandering road that tracks with you down the page. Topographic contour lines become tasteful decoration backing up the journey/map theme. It all works together to make navigating the page feel a little like taking a winding road trip. However, these little design flourishes don't for a moment detract from the great stories—both text and video—that you encounter as you scroll. This is rich, inventive, fun design.

## Users Can Move about Easily via Intuitive Navigation

We'll talk more about the placement of navigation later, but the main navigation block itself should be clearly visible on the page, and each link should have a descriptive title. A navigation structure that not only changes appearance when hovered over with the cursor, but also indicates the active page or section, helps users to recognize where they are, and how to get where they want to go. New Zealand renewables tech company [2] pinpoints your current location instantly in **For Home**, **E.Transport**, and **E-Scooters** in the example below.

---

[1] https://talltrueandtangled.com/
[2] https://www.mercury.co.nz/

1-3. Join the Electric Revolution

Secondary navigation, search fields, and outgoing links should not be dominant features of the page. If we make these items easy to find, and separate them visually from the content, we allow users to focus on the information—while they'll still know where to look when they're ready to move on to other content.

## Users Recognize Each Page as Belonging to the Site

Even if there's a dramatic difference between the layout of the home page and the rest of the site, a cohesive theme or style should exist across all site pages to help hold the design together. The supporting site for Russia's AZ Museum[3] slices and dices its layouts in lots of different ways, but there's no chance of becoming disoriented with that strong first column

3. https://museum-az.com/en/

navigation on every page.

1-4. Pages from the AZ Museum

## Web Page Anatomy

Even from a non-designer's standpoint, defining a design that satisfies all the requirements I outlined above is a simple task. It's similar to making a phrase on your refrigerator with magnetic poetry words. Although there are millions of ways to arrange the words, only a few arrangements make any sense. The magnetic words are like the components, or blocks, of the web page. Although the number of these necessary blocks depends on the size and subject of the site, most websites have the components seen below.

content from the bottom of the browser window, the footer should indicate to users that they're at the bottom of the page.

## Whitespace

The graphic design term **whitespace** (or **negative space**) refers to any area of a page without type or illustrations. While many novice web designers (and most clients) feel a need to fill every inch of a web page with photos, text, tables, and data, empty space on a page is every bit as important as content. Without carefully planned whitespace, a design will feel closed in, like a crowded room. Whitespace helps a design to *breathe* by guiding the user's eye around a page, but it also helps to create balance and unity—two important concepts that we'll discuss in more detail later in this chapter.

At this point, we've had our initial meeting with Mr. Smith, our theoretical client, and it was helpful. He explained very thoroughly what his business does and what he wants the site to achieve. Even though we've yet to see actual content, we can use the standard blocks of web page anatomy to start developing a layout. Although other site-specific blocks are worked into the designs of many website layouts, the web page anatomy works to summarize the most common blocks.

Now that we have this information, how can we use it to create a foundational layout for Smith's Services?

It's time for some grid theory.

## Grid Theory

When most people think about grids, they think about engineering and architecture. However, the grid is an essential tool for graphic design as well, and the use of grids in website design has exploded in popularity over the years.

Using a grid is more than simply making elements on the page square and lined up. It's about proportion as well. That's where the theory comes into grid usage. Many art historians credit Dutch painter Piet Mondrian as the father of graphic design for his sophisticated use of grids. Yet classical grid theory has influenced successful artistic efforts for thousands of years. The concept of dividing the elements of a composition extends back to the mathematical ideas established by Pythagoras and his followers, who defined numbers as ratios rather than single units.

The Pythagoreans observed a mathematical pattern that occurred so often in nature that they believed it to be divinely inspired. They referred to this pattern as the golden ratio or divine proportion. The basic idea is illustrated below.

1-6. The golden ratio

A line can be bisected using the golden ratio by dividing its length by 1.62. This magical 1.62 number is really 1.6180339 ..., an irrational number that's usually represented as Φ (pronounced "phi"). Explaining the math used to come up with this number is a bit too involved for this discussion, and is likely to be of no real help to you becoming a better designer, so I'll spare you the details. Besides, my math is a little rusty.

So just what does this ratio have to do with graphic design? In general, compositions divided by lines that are proportionate to the golden ratio are considered to be aesthetically pleasing. The artists of the Renaissance used divine proportion to design their paintings, sculpture, and architecture, just as designers today often employ this ratio when creating page layouts, posters, and brochures. Rather than relying on artistic judgement, divine proportion gives us logical guidelines for producing appealing layouts.

The aloe cactus pictured below[4] is an example of the golden ratio at work in nature. The scaling of each successive row of cactus spikes provides a perfect balance of spike placement and sun exposure.

[4.] Image Credit: Aloe Polyphylla: J Brew, 2005, https://flickr.com/photos/brewbooks/184343090

Golden ratio:

|←——————— 1.618 units ———————→|
| 0.618 unit | 1 unit |

1-7. Aloe polyphylla: the golden ratio in nature

This ratio thrives in good design. Movie posters like those featured below show how the golden ratio can be used as a way to both divide the canvas and position focal points. Keep in mind that these are useful guides, not irrefutable laws. The Ghostbusters poster clearly uses the golden ratio to size and position the red circle graphic, but the designers needed to bump that whole unit to the right slightly to balance the hand poking out on the left. If they'd perfectly centered that circle, the design would *feel* unbalanced.

1-8. The Usual Suspects and Ghosterbusters movie posters use the golden ratio in their layouts

## The Rule of Thirds

A simplified version of the golden ratio is the **rule of thirds**. A line bisected by the golden ratio is divided into two sections, one of which is approximately twice the size of the other. Dividing a composition into thirds is an easy way to apply divine proportion without your calculator.

For quick layout experimentation, I like to start off by drawing a bunch of simple rule-of-thirds grids with pencil and paper. Just draw a rectangle, divide it into thirds horizontally and vertically, then draw a line between each vertical line to create six columns to work within, as shown below.

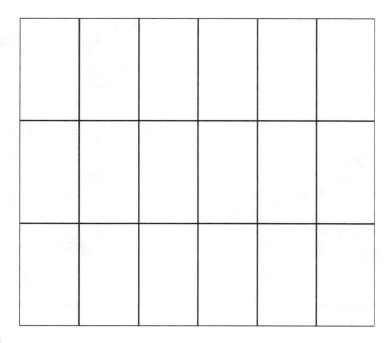

1-9. A simple grid

With this simple gridwork in place, we can begin to lay out our elements. This is often referred to as a "wireframe". **Wireframes** are simple sketches or layouts where you design blocks of content and their positioning on the page. Wireframes are extremely useful, because you can quickly and easily move elements around. The largest, outermost rectangle represents the container that we talked about in the section called "Web Page Anatomy". When using this method of layout design, I like to place the biggest block first. Usually, that block represents the content.

In my first rule-of-thirds grid, I place the content block within the two thirds of the layout at the lower right. Next, I place my navigation block in the middle third of the left-hand column. I place the text part of the identity block over the left side of the content, and the image part of the identity over the menu. Finally, I squash the copyright block below the content, in the right-hand column of the grid. The result is the top left of the four possible layout arrangements shown below.

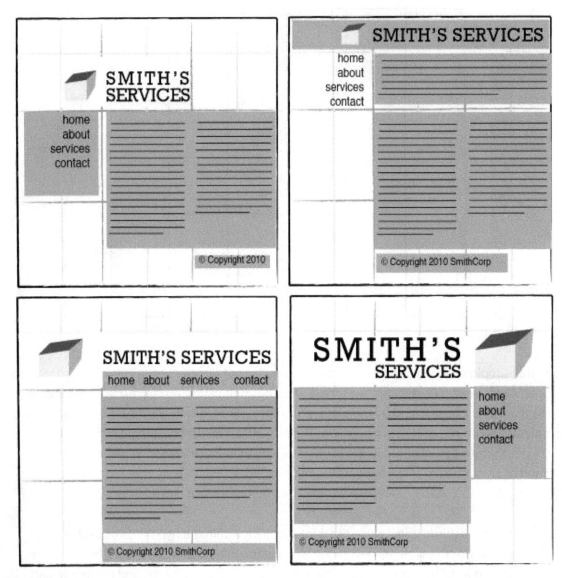

1-10. Four layouts in grids that follow the rule of thirds

These initial sketches provide a quick look into what general layout approaches might work for your website. No need to stop there, though. The growth in popularity of grid-based design on the Web has inspired many great articles about—and tools for—designing websites on a grid.

## CSS Frameworks

A CSS framework is a CSS system that is set up to handle the grid structure of a website. Most modern CSS frameworks are based on a 12-column grid, mostly because of the variety of column widths it offers, as twelve is divisible by 1, 2, 3, 4, and 6. Foundation[5], Bootstrap[6],

Bulma[7] and TailwindCSS[8] are all frameworks based on a 12-column grid—athough they can be customized to any number.

I usually start designing on a 12-column sketch sheet to make it easy to transition from my sketches and mockups to an actual working prototype. As you experiment with different arrangements for your own layouts, use the columns of whatever grid you've chosen as alignment guides for the identity, navigation, content, and footer blocks. It's very tempting to arrange all your elements within the same one or two blocks, but try to avoid this, as it's not very interesting visually. Instead, consider pushing some elements into another column or off the grid entirely.

One of the most common complaints you hear from new designers is that grids make designs too boxy and constrained. That's a cop-out. While grids can always suggest good positions to place elements, there's no reason to feel boxed in by them.

Take the design for **The Collective**[9] work/living spaces (below). The design uses lots of organic shapes and photo masks to create a quirky, flowing layout with very few square edges. However, roll a 14-column grid across it and the underlying structure becomes clearer. The two outer-most columns are treated mostly as text-free gutters, leaving a classic 12-column grid to divide up the remaining real estate. There's a lot of careful order and structure to this design, but it's skillfully obscured when you can't see the grid.

---

5. http://get.foundation/
6. http://getbootstrap.com/
7. https://bulma.io/documentation/
8. https://tailwindcss.com/
9. https://www.thecollective.com/

1-11. The Collective work/living spaces hides its grid well

Notice that, even in the naturally rectangular "locations" area at the bottom, the designers have used vertical offsets and irregular background shapes to camouflage any underlying blockiness.

To quote Josef Müller-Brockmann, graphic design pioneer (and author of *Grid Systems in Graphic Design*)[10]:

> *The grid system is an aid, not a guarantee. It permits a number of possible uses and each designer can look for a solution appropriate to his personal style. But one must learn how to use the grid; it is an art that requires practice.*

The longing we have for structure, grids, and ideal proportion is deeply ingrained in human nature. A layout that "doesn't look quite right" can often be fixed by moving elements and resizing them on the grid. So if a layout isn't working, keep experimenting. At some point, all

---

[10.] Josef Müller-Brockmann, *The Graphic Artist and His Design Problems*, Arthur Niggli Ltd, Switzerland, 1961, p92

the pieces will click together and the Tetris level-up sound will play in your head. You'll have achieved balance.

# Balance

In a figurative sense, the concept of **visual balance** is similar to that of physical balance illustrated by a seesaw. Just as physical objects have weight, so do the elements of a layout. If the elements on either side of a layout are of equal weight, they balance one another. There are two main forms of visual balance: symmetrical and asymmetrical.

## Symmetrical Balance

1-12. Examples of symmetrical balance

**Symmetrical balance**, or formal balance, occurs when the elements of a composition are the same on either side of an axis line, as shown below. The digital painting *Contemplation* by David Lanham, shown below, illustrates this concept well. Notice how the male and female figures are similar in position and proportion. Even the shaded background boxes are mirror images of one another.

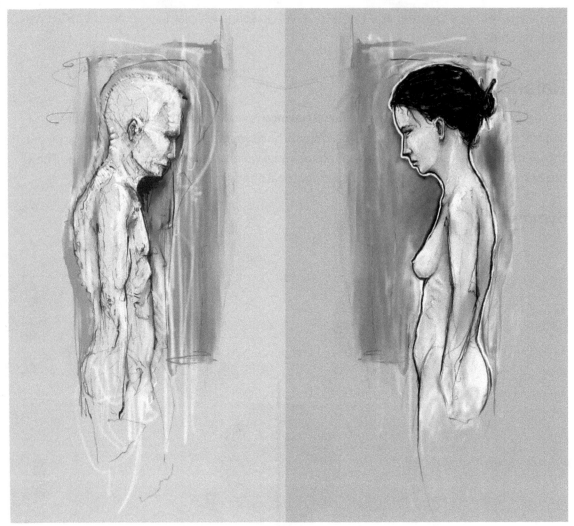

1-13. Symmetrical balance: Contemplation, by David Lanham

Although it may not be practical for all designs and clients, this type of symmetry—called **horizontal symmetry**—can be applied to website layouts by centering content or balancing it between equal columns. Momentum Energy[11] is an interesting example of using symmetry to balance their twin goals of sales and support. Notice on the screenshot below that they've halved the screen between a tagline/CTA (sales) on the left and major navigation (support) on the right. What's even more remarkable is the navigation list is the largest text on the screen. This is an unconventional design—perhaps even uncomfortable—but I suspect it's an earnest attempt to reduce human phone and email support costs.

---

[11] https://www.momentumenergy.com.au/

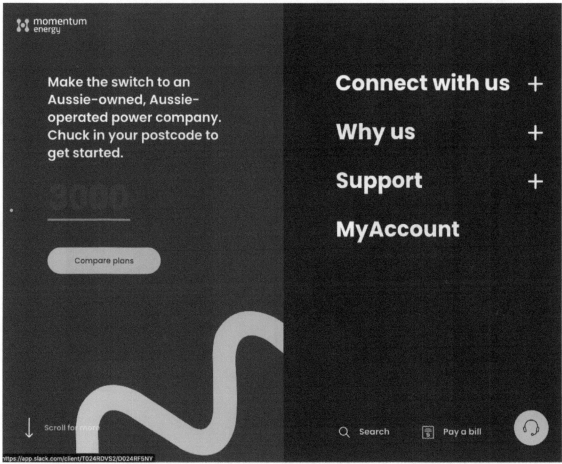

1-14. Momentum Energy

The two other forms of symmetrical balance are less common in website design, due to the nature of the medium. They are, however, commonly exhibited in logo and print design:

- **bilateral symmetry**, which exists when a composition is balanced on more than one axis
- **radial symmetry**, which occurs when elements are equally spaced around a central point

## Asymmetrical Balance

1-15. An example of asymmetrical balance

**Asymmetrical balance**, or informal balance, is a little more abstract (and more visually interesting in general) than symmetrical balance. An example of asymmetrical balance is shown above. Rather than mirror images on either side of the layout, asymmetrical balance involves objects of differing size, shape, tone, or placement. These objects are arranged so that, despite their differences, they equalize the weight of the page. For instance, if you have a large object on one side of a page, and partner it with several smaller items on the other side, the composition can still feel balanced.

The concert poster by my friend Jeremy Darty, presented below, is a fine example of asymmetrical balance. The visual weight of the large pink flamingo on the left is balanced by the combined weight of the smaller flamingos and text blocks on the right-hand side of the layout. Notice, also, Jeremy's use of the rule of thirds. The blue cloud behind the Pop Sucks title takes up one third of the vertical space and spans two thirds of the horizontal.

1-16. Asymmetrically balanced design by Jeremy Darty

Take a look at the photo of the three stones in the image below. It may not be a particularly exciting picture, but as far as balance goes, it rocks! If you were to use a piece of paper to cover any one of the three stones below, the entire photograph would feel unbalanced and unfinished. This is generally the way balance works. It's as if the entire composition is in a picture frame hanging by a single nail on the wall. It barely takes much weight on one side or the other to shift the entire picture off balance.

1-17. Asymmetrical rocks that don't roll

Unlike symmetrical balance, asymmetrical balance is versatile and, as such, is used more often on the Web. If you take a look at most two-column website layouts, you'll notice that the wider column is often lighter in color—a tactic that creates a good contrast for the text and main content. The smaller navigational column is often darker, has some sort of border, or is made to stand out in another way, in order to create balance within the layout.

The landing page for online mail service Handwrytten[12] shows how you can rebalance a page without needing to radically change the core content. Let's break it down. There are two major content areas on the page.

1   On the left, the Handwrytten logo, the tagline and the call to action are the first things they want you to notice.

2   On the right, they have visual demonstration of what the product *is*—a handwritten letter in an envelope. This service is a new concept, so it's important to show the actual product.

Their problem was that letters and envelopes are lightweight objects (visually and physically)

---

[12.] https://www.handwrytten.com/

and struggled to compete against the heavier tagline/CTA elements on the left. They needed some visual weight.

1-18. Handwrytten's designers engineered extra visual weight to create balance

No need to panic. As the figure above shows, Handwrytten's designers added two elements to the design:

1   They created a thick dark border on the letter.

2   They positioned a dark "hello" card behind the envelope to give it extra visual gravity.

Neither are critical to the page content, but the design becomes visually floaty and unmoored when I take them away.

# Unity

Design theory describes **unity** as the way in which the different elements of a composition interact with one another. A unified layout is one that works as a whole rather than being identified as separate pieces. Take the monkeys in the image below, for example. Their similarity of shape (not to mention their identical color) enables them to be recognized as a group, rather than as four disparate elements.

1-19. Rise up! Unity among the monkeys

Although less of an issue these days, unity is one of the many reasons web designers have always despised HTML frames. It's important that unity exists not only within each element of a web page, but across the entire web page. The page itself must work as a unit. We can use a couple of approaches to achieve unity in a layout (aside from avoiding frames): proximity and repetition.

## Proximity

**Proximity** is an obvious, but often overlooked, way to make a group of objects feel like a single unit. Placing objects close together within a layout creates a focal point towards which the eye will gravitate. Take a look at the digital painting below. While composed of a seemingly random assortment of strokes, the five strokes that are the closest to each other appear to form a unified object.

1-20. Creating a group using proximity

We practice the concept of proximity on the Web when we start setting margins and padding for elements. For instance, when I define the CSS style rules for sites, I usually change the default margin that exists between common HTML elements such as headings ( `h1` , `h2` , `h3` …), paragraphs, blockquotes, and even images. By altering these values, I can cause more or less space to appear between elements, thereby creating groups.

If you look at the two columns of text below, you'll notice that they look similar. The only difference is in the placement of the headings. In the column on the left, the word "Unkgnome" is equidistant from the top and bottom paragraphs. The result is that it looks more like a separator than a heading for the next paragraph. In the second column, the "Gnomenclature" heading is placed closer to the paragraph that follows it. In accordance with the rules of proximity, this heading appears to belong to that block of text.

1-21. Proximity between headers and content

## Repetition

A gaggle of geese, a school of fish, a pride of lions. Any time you bring a set of like items together, they form a group. In the same way, **repetition** of colors, shapes, textures, or similar objects helps to tie a web page design together so that it feels like a cohesive unit. The example below illustrates repetition. Even though other similar strokes exist, the nine red strokes on the left-hand side appear to be a unified group because they repeat a shape, color, and texture. The strokes to the right of this group have no repeated pattern, so they appear isolated, even though there are other shapes nearby.

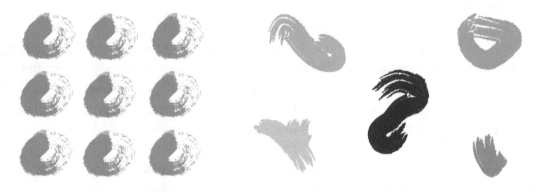

1-22. Creating a group using repetition

Whether you notice it or not, repetition is often used in website designs to unify elements of the layout. An example of this concept at work among unmodified HTML elements is the bulleted list. The bullet that precedes each list item is a visual indicator that the bullet items are parts of a whole. Repeated patterns and textures can also help to unify a design. Take a look at the screenshot of <u>Dribbble</u>[13], a hub for designers and developers to showcase and share their work. This layout contains many eye-catching elements, but the repeated thumbnail images with the views, comments and like icons create a sense of unity, while the navigation bar and the open content area give plenty of room to show off all of this awesome, unique design work.

---

13. https://dribbble.com/

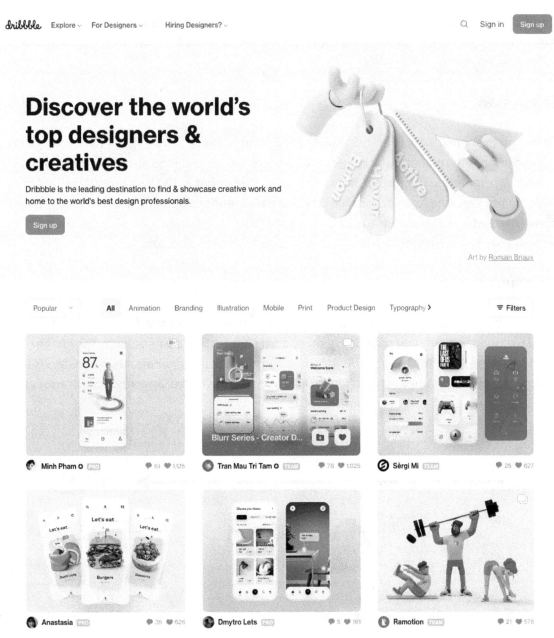

1-23. Dribbble home page

# Emphasis

Closely related to the idea of unity is the concept of emphasis or dominance. Rather than focusing on the various elements of a design fitting together, **emphasis** is about making a particular feature draw the viewer's attention. When you design a web page layout, often you'll identify an item in the content, or the layout itself, that you want to stand out. Perhaps it's a button for users to press, or an error message for them to read. One method of achieving such emphasis is by making that element into a focal point. A **focal point** is any element on a page that draws the viewer's eye, rather than just being part of the page as a whole or blending in with its surroundings. As with unity, there are a few tried-and-true methods of achieving a focal point.

## Placement

Although the constraints of practical web design don't often allow for it, the direct center of a composition is the point at which users look first, and is typically the strongest location for producing emphasis. The further from the center an element is, the less likely it will be noticed first. On the Web, the top-left corner of the page also tends to demand a lot of attention for those of us who read from left to right (remember that many languages, like Hebrew and Arabic, are read from right to left) and scan a page from top to bottom.

## Continuance

The idea behind **continuance** or **flow** is that when our eyes start moving in one direction, they tend to continue along that path until a more dominant feature comes along. The image below demonstrates this effect. Even though the bottom splotch is bigger and therefore tends to catch your eye first, your brain can't help but go "Hey, looky there, an arrow!" Soon enough, you'll find yourself staring at the smaller object.

1-24. Continuance and placement: creating emphasis

Continuance is one of the most common methods that web designers use to unify a layout. By default, the left edge of headings, copy, and images placed on a web page form a vertical line down the left side of a page before any styling is applied. A simple way to make additional use of this concept is to align elements to the lines of your grid. This creates multiple lines of continuance for your visitors' eyes to follow down the page.

The example below—a screenshot of the site of type agency <u>Bastarda</u>[14]—is a great example

---

14. https://www.bastardatype.com/

of continuance. Every curve, every echo drives your eye to the right, in this case for no particularly useful reason. In fact, this image is only one frame out of a <u>blipvert</u>[15] of images that Bastarda hammer you with on hover. It's very punk rock. Be warned.

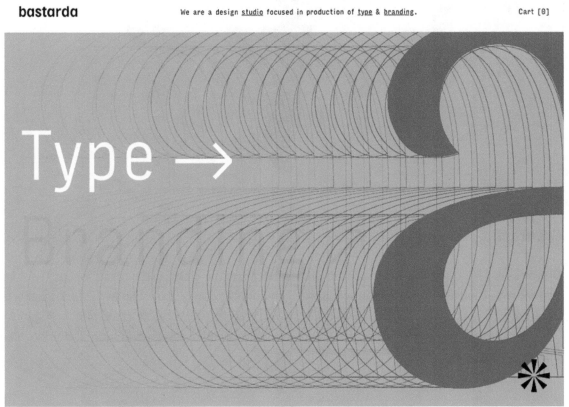

1-25. Continuance on Bastarda's site

## Isolation

In the same way that proximity helps us create unity in a design, **isolation** promotes emphasis. An item that stands out from its surroundings will tend to demand attention. Even though he's sad to be apart from his buddies, the isolated monkey below stands out as a focal point on the page.

---

15. https://tvtropes.org/pmwiki/pmwiki.php/Main/Blipvert

1-26. Isolation: a sad iso-monkey

## Contrast

**Contrast** is defined as the juxtaposition of dissimilar graphic elements, and is the most common method used to create emphasis in a layout. The concept is simple: the greater the difference between a graphic element and its surroundings, the more that element will stand out. Contrast can be created using differences in color (which I'll discuss in more detail in Chapter 2), size, and shape.

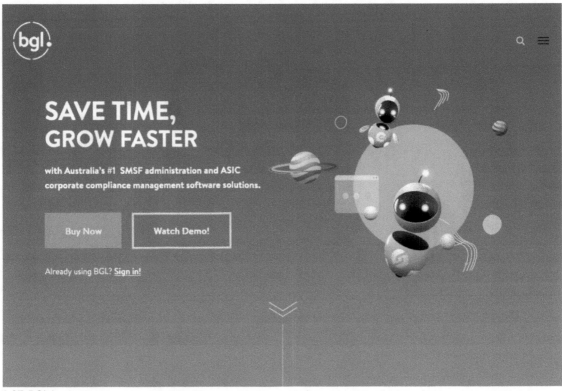

1-27. BGL home page

Take a look at the __BGL__[16] home page above. If there's one specific link or button you want your visitors to click, it's known as a **call to action (CTA)**. When you look at the design above, what first grabs your attention? For me, it's the **Buy Now** button on the left. It's the only place on the page that uses a warm color—a punchy orange against a calm sea of blues and greens. Of course, on a page of warm colors, a cool blue CTA would be high contrast.

## Proportion

Another interesting way of creating emphasis in a composition is through the use of proportion. **Proportion** is a principle of design that has to do with differences in the scale of objects. If we place an object in an environment that's of smaller scale than the object itself, that object will appear larger than it does in real life, and vice versa. This difference in proportion draws viewers' attention to the object, as it seems out of place in that context.

In te image below, I've taken our sad, isolated monkey and superimposed him over the skyline of Manhattan to prove my point. Between the sharp contrast in color and the difference in proportion, your brain immediately says, "Hey, this isn't quite right," and you're left staring at the monkey until you force yourself to look away.

16. https://www.bglcorp.com/

1-28. Proportion: a monkey in Manhattan

The Jim Beam Nigeria[17] website sets up a fairly conventional bar scene, but is a little more unorthodox with its hero shot. The bottle is scaled up, teetering at a precarious angle, and breaks through the hero panel borders. Further down, two glasses are shot from a completely different perspective, all designed to add some energy and life to the page.

---

17. http://jimbeamnigeria.com/

1-29. Jim Beam plays with scale and orientation

Creating emphasis in your design isn't just the key to making your call to action stand out. It's also how we move a viewer's eyes across the page. By giving elements a descending level of emphasis, you can suggest an order for visitors to follow. If you keep this in mind as you build your sites, you can echo the emphasis you create with semantic HTML markup and CSS. For instance, by matching `h1` to `h6` headline tags with a respective level of visual emphasis, you can provide a similar view of what's visually important in the page to search engines and vision-impaired visitors.

Next, we'll look at some tried and tested layout patterns you can borrow inspiration from.

# Bread-and-butter Layouts

Most of what we've talked about thus far has been design theory. Theory is helpful, but it can only take us so far towards understanding why some ideas work and others don't in a website's design. In my experience, examples and practice are much more valuable. Most academic graphic design programs include a curriculum that's rich in art history and fine art. These classes provide a great foundation for understanding graphic design from an art perspective, but they do little to prepare you for the specific challenges you'll encounter when you take your designs to the Web.

Pablo Picasso once said, *"I am always doing that which I cannot do, in order that I may learn how to do it."* While I like to take that approach when designing a new website, it's important first to know what you can do. When you look out across the Internet, you can see that the possibilities for layout are endless. Depending on the goals of the site, though, only a few of those possibilities make good design sense. That's why we see certain configurations of identity, navigation, and content over and over again.

In this section, we'll talk about the three most common layouts, and explore some of their advantages and disadvantages.

## Left-column Navigation

The left-column navigation pattern was arguably the design default for the first 15 years of the World Wide Web. Trawl the <u>web archives</u>[18] and you'll see that all the early incarnations of Yahoo!, AltaVista and Facebook leaned heavily on their left-column navigation. Today, it tends to be reserved for huge, link-heavy enterprise sites like Wikipedia or Craigslist.

---

18. http://web.archive.org

1-30. Moving through time: Alta Vista, Yahoo!, Facebook and Wikipedia with left-column navigation

To my eye, this format still *feels* old-fashioned and static—even in a bright, open design like the <u>Haywood Golf</u>[19] site (below)—so I tend to steer away from it. But that doesn't mean you have to. Left-column navigation is rare enough today that it might come off as cool and avant-garde if you get it right. It's always good to mix things up.

---

19. https://www.haywoodgolf.com/

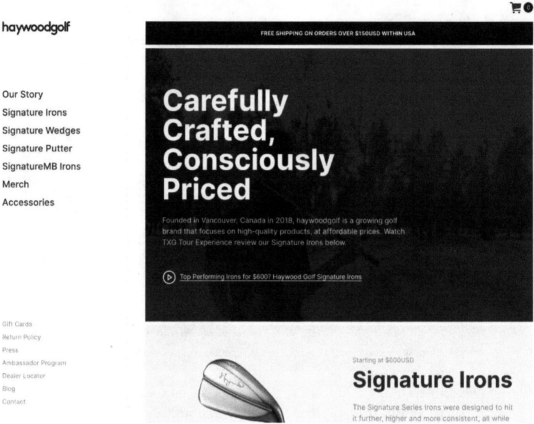

1-31. Haywood Golf home page

Speaking of mixing it up, how about picking that left column up and sticking it on the other side of the content? Then you'd have a right-column navigation layout.

## Right-column Navigation

If you're going to restrict your main content to one side of the page, it's not uncommon to push it to the left, placing navigation, advertising, and subsidiary content on the right. This prioritized content over navigation is a more common configuration for news sites (such as the Coda[20] example below), social networks such as Reddit[21], and websites with expansive navigation schemes that are unable to be contained within a simple top navigation.

---

20. https://www.codastory.com/
21. https://www.reddit.com

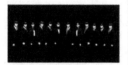
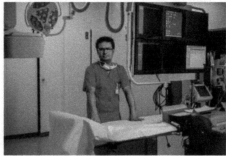

1-32. Right-column navigation at Coda

Ultimately, the decision on whether to put a navigation column on the left, the right or anywhere else is a judgment call that's really about the amount and type of content you have to organize. If it's a simple site that doesn't require any secondary navigation, consider a narrow, columnless layout. Good design is often more about what you leave out than what you put in.

If you do need a secondary column, just remember that the content is what your visitors are there for—and they're looking for it on the left first.

## Three-column Navigation

If you were paying attention to web design in the early 2000s, you may remember the obsession with "The Holy Grail Layout[22])"—a scaling, three-column layout with self equalizing column heights. Some of the world's greatest CSS minds[23] spent thousands of hours trying to force buggy browsers with primitive CSS support into reproducing a layout that had been

22. https://en.wikipedia.org/wiki/Holy_grail_(web_design)
23. https://alistapart.com/article/holygrail/

easy to do with HTML tables. It was like having all of NASA tasked with finding your house keys. Thanks, but *why is this so hard!?!*

The bitter irony is, today we have many elegant CSS Flexbox[24] and Grid[25] solutions to the Holy Grail, but far fewer opportunities to use them. Even big news sites such as CNN, The New York Times and BBC News prefer to use a broad header navigation followed by bite-sized content cards below. Today it's mostly social media sites like Twitter and Facebook carrying the classic three-column banner forward.

One notable exception is the dashboard for training app Strava[26] (you may have to log in to see the view in the image below). As a regular Strava user, I believe it's one of the best examples of how to present oceans of data in a layered, digestible, attractive way. If you're working on a complex UI problem, there's a lot you can learn from these guys.

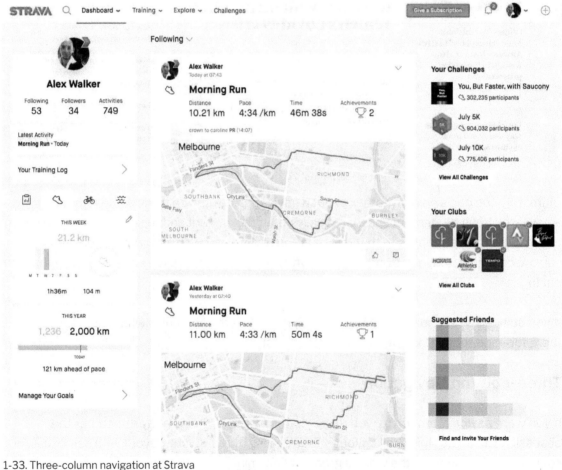

1-33. Three-column navigation at Strava

24. https://philipwalton.github.io/solved-by-flexbox/demos/holy-grail/
25. https://alligator.io/css/css-grid-holy-grail-layout/
26. https://www.strava.com/dashboard

## Navigationless Magazine Style

If you're reading this paragraph, I'm guessing you probably didn't arrive directly from the table of contents. On the Web, we tend to be a lot more goal-oriented and consume information in bits and pieces. Site navigation allows us to be quick, efficient … and erratic. What if you don't want your visitors skipping to another page? What if the information you need to convey is best consumed as a whole, like a book or magazine article? If that's the case, why include navigation at all? That's the approach that magazine sites like Typographica[27], Brand New[28], and Creative Review[29] take with each of their art-directed articles. Although technically you will find a line of text-link navigation on Typographica, it's so low-key as to be practically invisible.

[27]. https://typographica.org/
[28]. https://www.underconsideration.com/brandnew/
[29]. https://www.creativereview.co.uk/

1-34. Navigationless magazine style at Typographica

## Bare-bones Minimalism

Sharing a philosophical approach with the navigationless magazine style, many designers are focussing on a single task and simply removing all other distractions. Minimalist design is focussed on telling a sharply directed story, rather than offering the user lots of choice. You could think of this design approach as a "vertical slide deck" or Powerpoint style. San Francisco marketing outfit Matter Made[30] certainly takes this approach, limiting itself to tight messages in large font sizes and simple colors.

---

30. https://www.mattermade.co/

# Audacious goals, smashed.

From marketing strategy and leadership
through execution and results;
Matter Made produces reliable growth.

Former Andreessen Horowitz
Board Partner, and 3x CEO,
Dave Hersh on what it's like

1-35. Matter Made: is it a site or more of a vertical slide deck?

Minimalism isn't a new design trend by any stretch of the imagination—even on the Web. In the art world, the minimalist movement of the 1960s and '70s was a reaction against the overly self-expressive era of abstract expressionism. Similarly, the recent explosion in minimalism and single-page designs on the Web is a reaction against the overly interactive Web 2.0 era. It's an attempt at balancing out the hustle and bustle of social media with the equivalent of a peaceful café or quiet art gallery.

## Break the Mould Layouts

I created this category to encompass original web layout ideas that can't be easily shoehorned into any the earlier classifications.

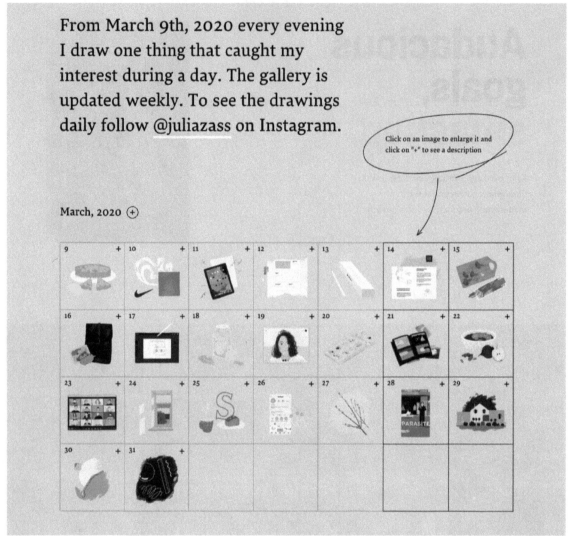

From March 9th, 2020 every evening I draw one thing that caught my interest during a day. The gallery is updated weekly. To see the drawings daily follow @juliazass on Instagram.

Click on an image to enlarge it and click on "+" to see a description

March, 2020 ⊕

1-36. Julia Zass's calendar UI is a great way to present her drawing-a-day project

Julia Zass is a talented illustrator who just needed a way to present and archive her "drawing-a-day" project. Her stripped-back UI is dominated by a handful of big calendars peppered with drawing thumbnails. It not only makes an attractive layout but also helps to explain the project at a glance—an elegant solution to a design problem.

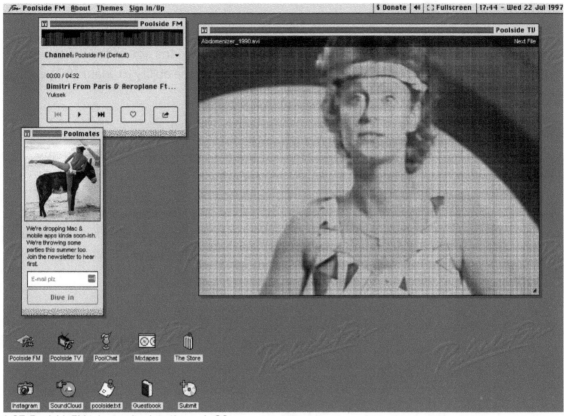

1-37. PoolsideFM take you back to the early 90s

"Elegant" is definitely *not* the word to describe <u>PoolsideFM</u>[31], a site that combines a sunny 90s soundtrack with dorky, unwanted 90s video clips in a mock Mac OS 8 interface. The UI lets you open and close desktop apps like you're using an old Apple computer. Sure, it's tongue-in-cheek, and I laughed the first time I loaded it. But here's the thing: it's hard to look away from those video clips. I still had the app open 20 minutes later. Does that make this a successful UI? Maybe. It's undoubtedly unique, quirky and fun.

I doubt we're looking at the next big design trend, but this aggressively original UI does its job!

## Web Trends

Every year, new techniques emerge. Many fade as quickly as they arrived—while a few become reliable, standardized techniques by employing new browser capabilities or new scripting breakthroughs. Let's run through a few.

---

[31] https://poolside.fm

## Video Backgrounds

The ability to play full-screen video backgrounds that respond to the size of the browser has been available to us for some time now, and certainly gives us the ability to adapt 100 years of cinema and television technique to the Web.

There are bandwidth issues to consider. Google's <u>WebM format</u>[32] provides impressive video compression, but isn't supported by all browsers, so you'll need to provide less efficient fallbacks for Safari.

There's also a question of whether auto-playing video is what your users want. Does a peak-hour subway commuter with a slow connection expect or want an auto-playing tennis shoe video as they browse for sports shoes? That's a question for "<u>The Roger</u>[33]", which uses some nicely edited video loops with its hero panel.

1-38. Video backgrounds in the The Roger

---

[32] https://www.webmproject.org
[33] https://theroger.com/

## Masonry Layouts

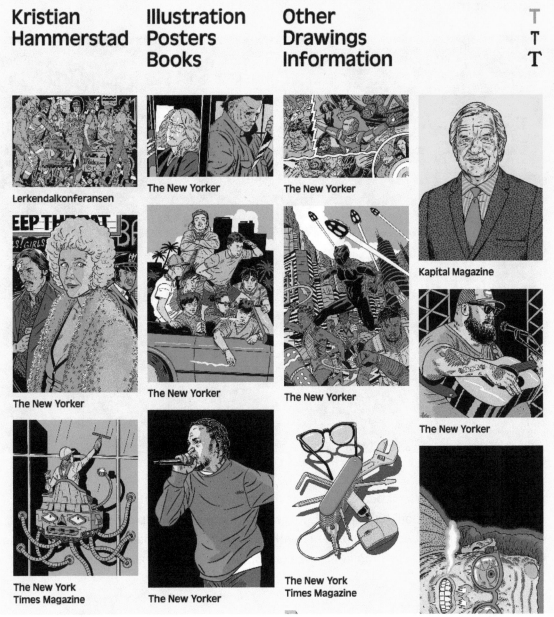

1-39. An example of Masonry layout

Another well-established trend is the Masonry[34] UI pattern. Masonry layouts stack content into equal-width columns while ignoring the idea of rows. Masonry is particularly well suited to arranging a collection of randomly sized images into a neat, easy-to-browse format. While Pinterest[35] is probably the poster child for Masonry, illustrator Kristian Hammerstad[36]

---

34. https://masonry.desandro.com/

(above) shows what a great showcase it provides for artwork and photography.

## Parallax Scrolling

1-40. Coros.net: Parallax in parall ... action?

Parallax scrolling began to appear in browsers around 2011, and within a few years it was overrunning the Web. Thankfully, these days it's more thoughtfully deployed. The concept uses stacked layers that scroll at different relative speeds, creating the illusion of depth in the viewport. Coros.net[37], shown above, is a nice example of parallax scrolling in action.

# Finding Inspiration

Just because the left-column, right-column, and three-column layout configurations are the bread and butter of most web page designs, there's no need to feel confined to these layouts. A plethora of design showcase and design pattern sites have been created to feature new and innovative ideas that might help you think outside the box, including those listed below (just

35. https://www.pinterest.com/
36. http://www.kristianhammerstad.com/
37. http://www.coros.net

to name a few).

- Awwwards[38] is a thoughtfully curated gallery of new site and app designs supported by an active and knowledgable community. The quality of nominees is generally high—outside of the occasional dodgy casino site.
- One Page Love[39] specializes in showcasing interesting, single-page website designs.
- Admire the Web[40] uses an easy-to-scan layout to put the spotlight on three or four newly launched sites every week. Always worth a look.
- Designspiration[41] continually curates galleries on a wide variety of design topics, from typography to photography, poster design, infographics and app design.
- OKMonk[42] is a relatively new but impressive site that bills itself as "a directory of quality UI/UX design resources". You're always a good chance to find new ideas on typography, tools, templates and more.
- The Inspiration Grid[43], although not strictly focussed on web/app design, hunts down eye-catching examples of typography, photography and graphic design that will stimulate your own new ideas.

## Using a Morgue File

I know what you're thinking: "Great, I have a bunch of galleries and pattern libraries to look at. Now what?" One of the most useful tips my first graphic design professor taught me was to create a **morgue file** whenever I was collecting inspiration for a large project. The concept is fairly simple: if you're doing an illustration or marketing project that involves trains, you clip out and print up anything you can find that might give you inspiration and keep it all in a folder. It helps with your current project, and should you ever need to do another project involving trains, you'll have lots of inspiration to hand.

The morgue file idea slipped my mind until a few years ago. I was looking for a site I'd seen in a favorite gallery site, but I couldn't remember the site's name or address. Doubtless it's great to have access to lots of inspirational resources, but they're useless if you can't find the specific example you're looking for. That was when I started my own digital morgue file. Having a repository of website designs that I can look at has been a handy resource on countless occasions when I've been searching for inspiration.

---

38. https://www.awwwards.com
39. https://onepagelove.com/
40. https://www.admiretheweb.com/
41. https://www.designspiration.com/
42. https://okmonk.com/
43. https://theinspirationgrid.com/

**Capture a Screenshot for Your Own Morgue File**

1    Select the browser window that's displaying the page you want to save as a screenshot.

2    Copy a screenshot of the browser window to your clipboard:

3    On a PC, press `Alt+Print Screen` or use the native Snipping Tool in Windows to grab a section of the screen. On a Mac, press `Shift+Command+4`, then `Space` to turn the cursor into a camera. Then, hold down `Ctrl`, and click on the browser window.

4    At this point, you should have a screenshot of the browser window in your clipboard. Open a new document in your favorite graphics program or document editor, and paste in the screenshot.

5    Save your image or document.

# Responsive Design

We can't really discuss layout without talking about how the design will be displayed on various screens. Responsive design allows us to craft designs that work not just on mobile phones, tablets and desktops, but TVs, fridges and AR goggles. Before the birth of responsive design, building for mobile devices meant designing standalone sites for smaller screen sizes—the short-lived era of the "m-dot" site. Ethan Marcotte's 2010 article[44] was the first to seriously describe a process that allowed us to build a single application that looks native on all devices. With the continued growth of mobile technology, there's now every reason to believe that at least half your audience is mobile. No organization can afford to neglect half its audience.

 **Are Standalone Mobile Sites Still a Thing?**

It's interesting to note that both Twitter (mobile.twitter.com) and Facebook (m.facebook.com) still redirect their mobile traffic to a separate mobile site as of 2020. However, they remain the exceptions amongst the internet giants, with everyone from Amazon to Microsoft, eBay, Instagram and Spotify choosing to build a unified web application that is responsive from the ground up.

---

44. https://alistapart.com/article/responsive-web-design/

# Screen Resolutions

Let's start with a look at the current state of screen resolutions. Over the last 20 years, screen resolutions and physical sizes have diversified tremendously.

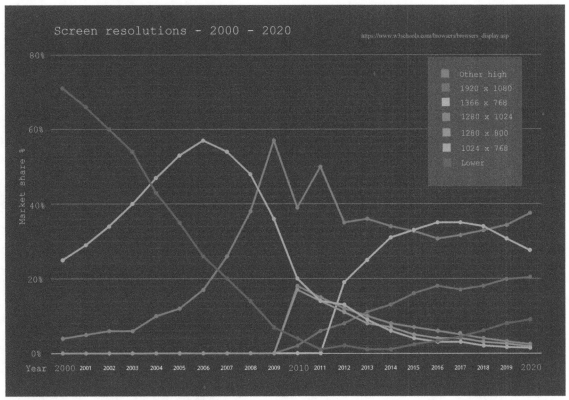

1-41. W3Schools' screen resolution statistics, 2000–2020, source: https://www.w3schools.com/browsers/
browsers_display.asp/

Let's look at some of the interesting numbers shown in the figure above:

- Our jobs were much simpler in the early 2000s, when two screen sizes comprised 90% of the browser market.
- Growth in high-resolution screens was explosive until around 2009, when the rise of iOS and Android began to move users onto mobile in large numbers.
- Low resolution screens (below `1024px`) have been in steep decline for most of the past two decades, but we've seen a recent rebound—likely due to lower-resolution phones.
- W3Schools caters strongly to developers, so it's likely their traffic is more desktop-centric than the average website.

It's also worth noting that many users with larger monitors tend not to maximize browser windows, so they can see other applications they have running.

## How Do @media Queries Work?

Responsive design uses CSS to control which rules are applied based on the screen size of the device displaying it. One way of doing this is with **media queries**. The site is instructed to determine a device's screen resolution. In the stylesheet, you create **breakpoints**, which are used to specify the size and structure of elements depending on the screen width of the device. These breakpoints are ranges of pixel widths for the different screen sizes you wish to target. For example, you may set breakpoints for mobile devices from `0px` to `568px`. The CSS to set this particular breakpoint would look something like this:

```
@media only screen and (min-device-width: 320px) and (max-device-width: 568px) {
  ...
}
```

Then, you may set the next breakpoint to a range that fits most tablet devices, and then desktop. The advantage of using breakpoints and media queries is that you can set as many breakpoints as you want.

The truth is, the topic of responsive design is far too deep to fit within the scope of this book, so if you want to go deep on the technical aspects, here's your reading list:

- the seminal "Responsive Web Design"[45] article by Ethan Marcotte
- *Jump Start Responsive Web Design, 2nd Edition*[46] by Chris Ward
- *Responsive Design*[47] by John Rhea

However, let's next look at the pure design considerations of responsive web design.

# Responsive Web Design Principles

How should a designer approach designing a responsive application?

## Always Design for "Mobile First"

Nearly all of the earliest responsive websites were "desktop first" designs. This meant that developers usually took their existing, fully featured desktop sites and then used CSS `@media` queries to *add more CSS* when the browser detected the screen was small. This was understandable but not a great experience. The idea of trying to simplify anything by adding

---

[45.] https://alistapart.com/article/responsive-web-design/
[46.] https://www.sitepoint.com/premium/books/jump-start-responsive-web-design-2nd-edition/
[47.] https://www.sitepoint.com/premium/books/responsive-design

more to it is rarely a good recipe for success.

**Mobile first** is the principle of making the default view of your layout a simple, fast-loading, mobile-friendly design, and then using `@media` queries to add on any richer, perhaps heavier page elements only when the browser conditions make sense. This makes sense not only from a screen-size perspective, but also from the perspective of mobile bandwidth limits.

## Don't Jam Elements into the Mobile View

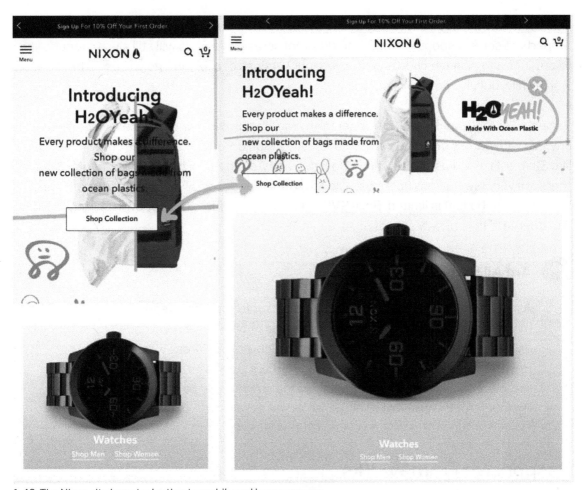

1-42. The Nixon site layout adapting to mobile and larger screens

In the Nixon.com[48] example above, you'll notice they don't render the "H2OYeah!" logo in the mobile view. That's not because it has no value. Bags made from recycled ocean trash is an excellent sales point. The problem is, jamming it into the mobile view compromises everything else:

---

48. https://www.nixon.com/us/en

- the watch gets pushed down and off screen
- the bag graphic gets more obscured
- the "Shop Collection" button has more visual competition

Nixon have been pragmatic enough to realize that shoehorning it into the mobile design isn't an overall win.

## SVG Is Your BFF

While there's a lot of great information on using the `picture` element and the `srcset` property to serve responsive images to different screen sizes, this will still always require you to produce and manage two, three or even four versions of every image you use. That's worthwhile, but also no small undertaking.

Scalable Vector Graphics (SVGs) render in any modern browser and can scale up or down to any size with no loss of image quality, so a single graphic works in all screen sizes. Today, apps like Sketch, Figma, Illustrator, Affinity Designer and Adobe XD all produce beautiful SVGs, so there are very few reasons not to use the format in your designs whenever practical. Even if your software budget is limited, Boxy SVG[49] has some abilities that not even Sketch or Figma can offer—for the princely sum of $9.

 **Are All SVG Files Small?**

As the name suggests, SVG is primarily a vector format that creates imagery from mathematics and geometry rather than a grid of pixels (like JPEG and PNG, for example). This can be a very efficient way to cover large areas with imagery. However, it's possible to import PNG and JPEG graphics into SVG. While this is sometimes useful, you're also importing the natural file size issues and scaling limitations of the pixels of all bitmaps.

# Responsive Frameworks

If you're not interested in coding your own responsive layout from scratch, your safest option is to adopt one of the established responsive frameworks—Foundation or Bootstrap.

Foundation[50], shown below, is a mobile framework by Zurb that's packed with tons of web development features. It currently weighs in at around 60KB of CSS and 84KB of JavaScript,

---

49. https://boxy-svg.com/
50. https://get.foundation

but this can be trimmed substantially by removing components you don't need. Later, if you need to add extra features such as responsive navigation menus, image sliders, accordion menus, validated forms, buttons, model popups, panels, tooltips, progress bars, or responsive tables, you know the components will be responsive.

There's also a nice feature that lets you generate working prototypes quickly.

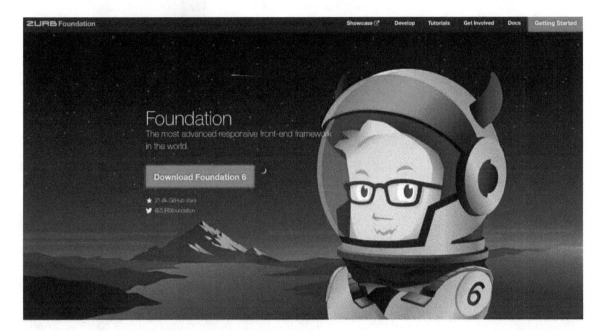

1-43. The Foundation 6 framework

Bootstrap[51], shown below, is the other framework battling for the number-one spot as the responsive framework of choice. Much like Foundation, Bootstrap has a number of its own built-in components that allow you to quickly create well-structured, mobile-first websites. Bootstrap has plenty of integrated features that are comparable to Foundation. With Bootstrap, you can create jumbotrons, panels, wells, navigation bars, progress bars, dropdowns, badges, alerts, tooltips, popups, tabs, carousels, and much more. Bootstrap also integrates the use of **glyphicons**, an embedded font library for use with the framework.

---

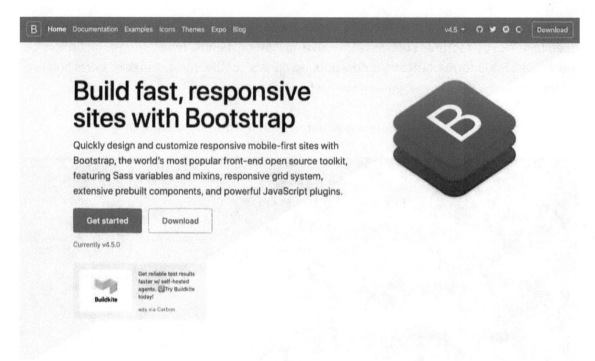

1-44. The Bootstrap framework

The primary reason people love Foundation and Bootstrap is that they're highly customizable. You don't have to download or even include the JavaScript files for components you aren't using. Simply click the checkboxes corresponding to the components you need, and leave the ones you don't. And once you've made your selections, Foundation and Bootstrap can compile them into custom downloads. They essentially take all the hard work out of compiling the components of your web development project.

With developers keen to create the leanest websites possible, with the least amount of JavaScript, and the smallest file sizes, it's easy to see why this approach is so popular.

One issue that's arisen with responsive web design is that traditional navigation menus don't always work the same way on a mobile device as they do on a desktop screen. When there isn't enough screen real estate, things can become jumbled. The solution that's been widely adopted is the mobile or "hamburger" menu. It's an icon of three lines stacked vertically, as shown in the top-right of the figure below, that represents an expandable menu, only available when the icon is tapped. The menu contents then appear as an overlay on top of the site's content.

1-45. A Foundation menu on a desktop screen

The menu shown above is how the menu in Foundation looks on the desktop. On a mobile device, such as a phone or a tablet, the menu is collapsed until you interact with it, such as in the examples shown below.

1-46. A Foundation menu on a mobile display

# The Project: Trashmonger

To walk you through the main design concepts we're talking about, it's helpful to have a real-world project to apply them to. For this book, that project will be "Trashmonger". My partner, Trish, is a photographer/digital artist and is looking to create a simple, attractive gallery site to display and market her work. Clearly there will be plenty of imagery that we don't want it to distract from, but the site needs to be attractive, memorable and professional. Her visual style is a blend of abstract modern and pop art, so we'll need to honor that in the design.

## Assets

It's always good to start with a stocktake to help understand your strengths, your weak points, and what you're currently missing. At the beginning of the projects I have:

- a working logo
- 25+ art pieces
- 100+ photographs

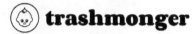

**trash** [noun]. pl.
discarded. thrown away

**monger** [noun].
a dealer in or trader of a commodity

Font: Corben bold

1-47. Assets for the site: logo, images, fonts and some definitions

Currently, we don't have any written supporting content, so I'll need to get that moving along in parallel to the design.

## Requirements

Looking at requirements, I think we have four basic page types:

- a landing/home page
- a gallery page, displaying a body of work
- product pages that show off individual pieces
- utility pages, for information such as about us, contact, and privacy

We'll also have external paths to Instagram and a shopping cart. Things may change as the project evolves, but we're going to start with this sitemap.

# Sitemap

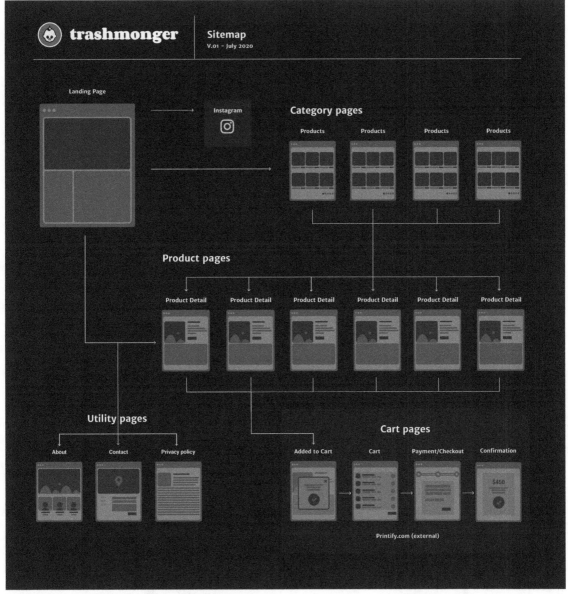

1-48. The first version of the Trashmonger sitemap

**Choosing a UI Design Tool**

The first edition of this book (published in 2005) focused on using Adobe Photoshop for most design tasks. While Photoshop is a magnificent photo editor, UI design has moved on to more specialised tools. I'm going to focus on three:

- Figma[52]
- Sketch[53]
- Adobe XD[54]

Each of these applications gives you the ability to create reusable **symbols** (or **components** in Figma) that let you generate child components based on a single parent component. Changes made to the parent automatically flow through to all the child components. This is perfect for creating the kind of generic interface units you need for wireframe designs.

It's true that there are many good specialist wireframing tools such as Balsamiq,[55] Moqups[56] and HotGloo[57]. Certainly check them out, but unless you're spending most of your week wireframing, I suspect most of your wireframing needs will be covered by one of the general editors listed above.

I'm a big advocate for Figma and will be using it for the sitemap (pictured above), the wireframes, and also the finished Trashmonger designs.

## Wireframes

The 12-column layout has been the default desktop configuration for more than a decade. Kicking off with 960Grid[58], and carried forward with Bootstrap and Foundation, 12 is a super versatile number to work with, as it breaks neatly into halves, thirds, quarters, and sixths.

Having said that, we're *not* going to use a 12-column layout in our example. Instead, we're going to change things up a little and design around a five-column layout. Why would we do that?

I find there's often extra energy in odd-numbered column layouts. You can get a sense of this

---

[52.] https://www.figma.com
[53.] https://www.sketch.com/
[54.] https://www.adobe.com/products/xd.html
[55.] https://balsamiq.com/
[56.] https://moqups.com
[57.] https://www.hotgloo.com/
[58.] https://960.gs/

by comparing the four-column and five-column layouts below. Even numbered columns can be so evenly balanced that they lack natural flow and movement.

1-49. Even-numbered vs odd-numbered columns

By comparison, the five-column layout seems to naturally "hang" from its center column like a trunk. That middle column is often the easiest path into the layout, and I want to use that natural flow in this design. A five-column layout can also be broken down into a handful of useful variations: 4–1, 3–2, 2–3, and 1–4.

Here are the basic wireframes for the Home page and the Product page including a mobile rendering.

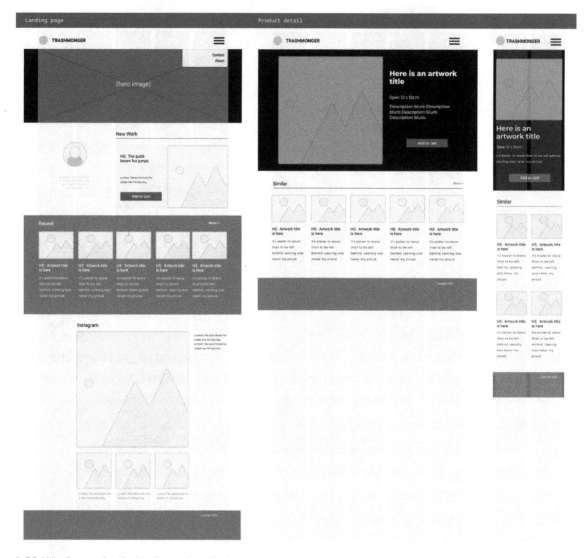

1-50. Wireframes for the landing and product pages

The Home page has more to accomplish, so is necessarily more complex. It needs to:

- welcome and orient users
- spotlight the latest work
- offer paths to other work
- set a visual style/tone

The Product detail page can have a narrower focus so can be simpler:

- showcasing the selected artwork
- offering paths to a handful of alternative art pieces

I tend to keep my wireframes to monotone for everything except call-to-action buttons (CTAs). I find emphasizing CTAs in wireframes helps keep them front of mind when you're making layout design decisions later.

So these are the bones that we get to flesh out. Our next consideration is the palette we're going to use. So in the next chapter, we'll talk about color.

Color | Chapter
2

Whether you're defusing a ticking time bomb, or trying to design a decent-looking site, if you choose the wrong color, you're doomed. Okay, so the wrong color selection for a client's site is unlikely to be the death of you, but it could curtail your budding career as a web designer. Choosing colors is no simple matter. There are aesthetic, identity, and usability considerations to take into account. And, to make matters worse, most modern displays can render more than sixteen million colors. That's a huge number of horrible color combinations just waiting to happen!

Fortunately, there's no need to be a swatchbook-carrying color consultant to make good color choices. A wealth of knowledge is available, from touchy-feely (as I like to call them) psychological guidelines to tried-and-true color theories that will help you make the right choices with your palette.

# The Psychology of Color

Color psychology is a field of study that's devoted to analyzing the emotional and behavioral effects produced by colors and color combinations. Ecommerce website owners want to know which color will make their website visitors spend more money. Home decorators are after a color that will transform a bedroom into a tranquil Zen retreat. Fast-food restaurant owners are dying to know which color combinations will make you want to super-size your meal. As you can imagine, color psychology is big business.

Although it's important to know how your color choices might affect the masses, the idea that there's a single, unified, psychological response to specific colors is spurious. Many of the responses that color psychologists accredit to certain colors are rooted in individual experience. It's also interesting to note that many cultures have completely different associations with, and interpretations of, colors. With those caveats in mind, let's explore some general psychological associations that the majority of people in Western cultures have in response to specific colors.

## Color Associations

Describing the emotional connections that people can have with colors can be a very hippy-esque topic. If you find that hard to believe, just head over to your favorite online music store and sample some tracks from *Colors*, by Ken Nordine. Although most designers will stop short at relying solely on the supposed meanings, characteristics, and personalities of specific colors, it's still handy to have an understanding of the emotional attributes of some of the main color groups. It's also important to keep in mind that color associations should be considered in context with their culture.

## Red

The color red has a reputation for stimulating adrenaline and blood pressure, and is also known to increase human metabolism. It's an exciting, dramatic, and rich color. Red is also a color of passion. Nothing says love quite like painting a wall bright red on Valentine's Day for your sweetheart, as seen below. The darker shades of red, such as burgundy and maroon, have a rich, indulgent feeling about them—the flip side of which is that they have the potential to seem quite hoity-toity. Think about these colors when designing anything for wine enthusiasts or connoisseurs of fine living. The more earthy shades of red are associated with autumn and harvest time.

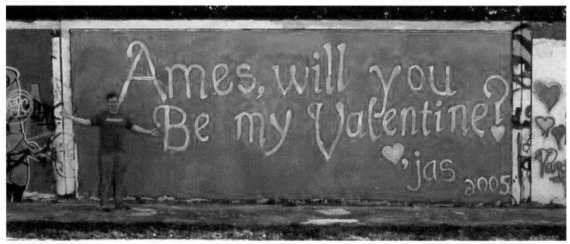

2-1. Red, the color of affection (two gallons of it!)

## Orange

Like red, orange is an active and energetic color, although it doesn't evoke passion in the way red can. Orange is thought to promote happiness, and represents sunshine, enthusiasm, and creativity. Orange is a more informal and less corporate-feeling color than red, which is perhaps a reason why the designers behind the operating system Ubuntu chose it for their logo. Since orange is a relatively rare sight in nature, it tends to jump out at us when we see it. For that reason, it's often used for objects that require high visibility, such as life jackets, road cones, and hunting vests. Orange, like red, also stimulates metabolism and appetite, so it's a great color for promoting food and cooking. That's probably why the picture of a tangerine below is making you hungry, even if you don't like citrus fruits.

2-2. Orange you glad I didn't say banana?

## Yellow

Like orange, yellow is an active color, and being highly visible, it's often used for taxicabs and caution signs. It's also associated with happiness and, as the image below illustrates, is the signature color of smileys. The original orange and lemon-lime flavors of the sports energy drink Gatorade are still the brand's best-selling products. This is likely due—at least partly—to the energetic characteristics associated with the colors orange and yellow.

2-3. Yellow, the color of smileys

An anonymous quote that's often used with color associations says, "Babies cry more in yellow rooms, husbands and wives fight more in yellow kitchens, and opera singers throw more tantrums in yellow dressing rooms". Whether true or not, the point is that too much yellow can be overpowering. Come on—if you were a baby stuck in a dressing room with fighting spouses and tantrum-throwing opera singers, you'd cry too!

## Green

Green is most commonly associated with nature. It's a soothing color that symbolizes growth, freshness, and hope. There's little doubt why the color has been so closely tied with environmental protection. Visually, green is much easier on the eyes, and far less dynamic, than yellow, orange, or red. Although many website designs using green appeal to visitors' sense of nature, green is a versatile color that can also represent wealth, stability, and education. When bright green is set against a black background, it really pops—lending the design a technological feel. For me, it brings back memories of my first computer—a trusty old Apple IIe. This was the inspiration for the MailChimp loading screen I designed, shown below.

2-4. ASCII version of Freddie Von Chimpenheimer IV

## Blue

When I was a kid, my favorite color was blue. Not just any blue, but cerulean blue from Crayola crayons. While most kids are less particular about the particular shade, blue is often cited as a universally loved color. On the touchy-feely level, blue symbolizes openness, intelligence, and faith, and has been found to have calming effects. On the other hand, blue has also has been found to reduce appetite. This is probably due, in part, to the rarity of blue in real food. Aside from blueberries, how many naturally blue foods can you count? Blue, it would seem, is excluded from nature's appetite-inducing palette. As such, it's less than ideal for promoting food products.

In addition, blue is sometimes seen as a symbol of bad luck and trouble. This emotional color connection is evident in blues music, as well as in the paintings of Picasso's depression-induced "blue period". It's not all about unnatural food colors and melancholy forms of art, though. Blue has universal appeal because of its association with the sky and the sea. For me, the presence of blue in the stacked stones image below makes me feel more at ease.

2-5. Calming stones, sky, and sea

This visual connection makes blue an obvious choice for websites associated with airlines, air conditioning, pool filters, and cruises. Have you ever noticed that blue is the primary color in the logos of IBM, Dell, HP, and Microsoft? That's because blue also conveys a sense of stability and clarity of purpose ... that is, until you've experienced the dreaded blue screen of death!

## Purple

Historically, the color purple has been associated with royalty and power, as it is on the postage stamp below. The secret behind purple's prestigious past has to do with the difficulty of producing the dye needed to create purple garments. To this day, purple still evokes wealth and extravagance. That extravagance is carried over into nature. Purple is most often connected with flowers, gemstones, and wine. It balances the stimulation of red and the calming effects of blue. According to Patrick McNeil, author of *The Web Designer's Idea Book*[1], purple is one of the least-used colors in web design. He explains that finding good examples of website designs featuring purple was so hard that he almost had to cut the section from his book. If you're trying to create a website design that stands out from the crowd, think about using a rich shade of purple.

---

[1] Patrick McNeil, *The Web Designer's Idea Book*, How Books, Cincinatti, USA, 2008

2-6. Purple coat of arms on a Norwegian postage stamp

## White

You might think there's nothing special about the color of the wind turbines below, but the use of white actually helps to promote the idea that this is clean power. In Western cultures, white is considered to be the color of perfection, light, and purity. This is why crisp white sheets are used in detergent commercials, and why a bride wears a white dress on her wedding day. For an idea of how ingrained the meaning of white is in our culture, read the poem *Design*[2]>, by Robert Frost. In it, Frost symbolically contradicts our associations by using white to represent death and darkness. Interestingly, in Chinese culture, white is a color traditionally associated with deaths and mourning. Such cultural distinctions should serve as a reminder to research the color associations of your target audience, as they may vary greatly from your own.

In design, white has been overlooked because it's the default background color of paper and screens. But as the rise of "Dark mode" has shown, you don't need to be afraid to shake it up. Try using dark or charcoal backgrounds with white text, or put a white background block on an off-white canvas to make it pop. Using colors in unexpected ways can make a bold statement.

---

[2] This can be found in many a good poetry book, but I used *The Norton Anthology of Poetry* (5th edition), eds Margaret Ferguson, Mary Jo Salter, and Jon Stallworthy, WW Norton & Company, New York, 2004.

2-7. These wind turbines might be white, but they're also green

## Black

Although black often suffers from negative connotations such as death and evil, it can also be a color of power, elegance, and strength, depending on how it's used. If you're wondering what the associations are for a particular color, just ask yourself, "What are the first three things that come to mind when I think about it?" For me, black conjures mental images of Johnny Cash, tuxedos, and Batman. Cash, in particular, is a powerful emotional trigger, with his black clothes, deep voice and melancholy songs.

2-8. Black, a color that represents power, elegance, and in this case, exorbitance

If you treat all your color choices this way, establishing three word associations for each, chances are you'll gain a good idea of how that color is widely perceived among your audience.

Even though color psychology plays a role in the way a visitor may see your site, keep in mind there's no wrong color to use. While psychological reasoning may help to start your palette, the success of a color scheme depends on the harmony that exists between all the colors you choose. To achieve this, we'll need to be mindful of a few other attributes of color.

## Color Temperature

One such attribute that exists across the entire spectrum is color temperature. Which color faucet gives you hot water? What color do you associate with ice? Why? The answers are obvious, and are enforced by both culture and nature.

WARM COLORS

2-9. The range of warm colors

**Warm** colors are the colors from red to yellow, including orange, pink, brown, and burgundy. Due to their association with the sun and fire, warm colors represent both heat and motion. When placed near a cool color, a warm color will tend to pop out, dominate, and produce the visual emphasis that we talked about in Chapter 1.

COOL COLORS

2-10. The range of cool colors

**Cool** colors are the colors from green to blue, and can include some shades of violet. Violet is the intermediary between red and blue, so a cooler violet is, as you'd imagine, one that's closer to blue, while a reddish violet can feel warm. Cool colors are calming, and can reduce tension. In a design, cool colors tend to recede, making them great for backgrounds and larger elements on a page, since they won't overpower your content.

## Chromatic Value

The measure of the lightness or darkness of a color is known as its **chromatic value**. Adding white to a color creates a **tint** of that color. Likewise, a **shade** is produced by adding black to a given color. Adding the complementary color will produce a shade that's more lifelike and natural. This method is often used in painting, because it won't be quite as dark. This figure illustrates this distinction.

2-11. Chromatic value

As with colors themselves, the chromatic value of colors you're using can impact on the psychological connection users will have to the content. One use of chromatic value might be to accent the time of day that customers associate with a company or organization. If you were designing a website that's all about nightlife or concerts, for instance, you'd probably want to go with dark shades and limit your use of light tints.

Tints tend to be associated with daylight, springtime, and childhood. Think sunrise, baby clothes, and Care Bears. These light pastel colors can be used in professional, sophisticated, grown-up ways, too, as anyone who's ever spent time in a hospital can attest. This is because tints are soothing colors that provide personality to sterile environments without startling the ill or making babies cry. Color designers are generally uninspired by colors such as "Hospital Green," but if you're working on a website for a day spa, tints would be a great foundation for your color palette.

### Saturation

The **saturation** or **intensity** of a color is described as the strength or purity of that color. It's obvious that intense, vivid colors stand out. Even though cool colors tend to recede, a vivid blue will draw more attention to itself than a dull orange. When we add gray (black and white) to a color, it becomes dull and muted. Like an office with beige walls, or an overcast winter morning, these colors are less exciting or appealing than bright, vivid colors. On the bright side—no pun intended—dull colors help to reduce tension, giving compositions a meditative, dreamy mood.

The relationship between value and saturation is illustrated below.

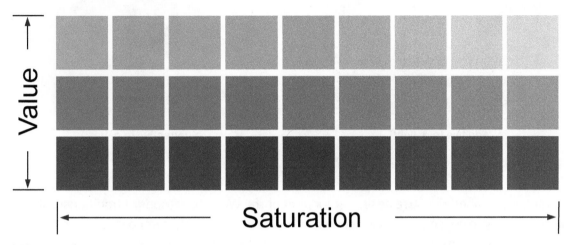

2-12. Value and saturation chart

## Color Theory 101

To take our knowledge of color further, we'll first need to gain a grounding in some of the more technical concepts associated with the subject, such as how colors are formed and how they can be categorized.

The colors displayed on your computer screen (that is, the colors we'll be using in our website designs) are based on an additive color model. In an **additive** color model, colors are displayed in percentages of red, green, and blue (RGB) light. If we turn all three of these colors on full blast, we'll have white light. If we turn red and green all the way up, but switch off blue, we have yellow.

If you've ever owned a color printer, you might be familiar with the acronym CMYK (cyan, magenta, yellow, and black). Your inkjet printer, laser printer, and industrial four-color printing press all create images using cyan, magenta, yellow, and black inks or toners. This process uses a **subtractive** color model. By combining colors in this color model, we come close to achieving a grayish black. There's no way of producing black combining just cyan, magenta, and yellow. This is why they're always supplemented with black—the K in CMYK. Take a look below for a better idea of how additive and subtractive color models work.

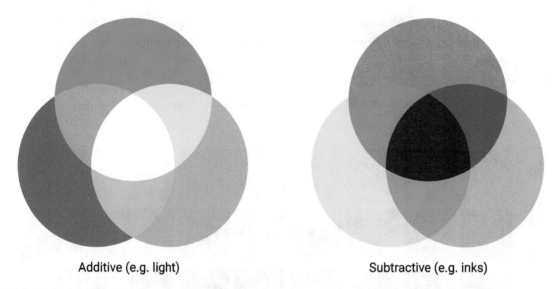

Additive (e.g. light)                Subtractive (e.g. inks)

2-13. RGB additive color model (left) and the CMYK subtractive color model (right)

Regardless of whether you're designing for print or the Web, the lessons of traditional color theory are key to helping us classify colors and group them together. Recorded studies of color classification date back to the fourth century BC and the works of Aristotle. Since then, many other great artists and philosophers have contributed to our knowledge of how colors work, including Isaac Newton, Johann Wolfgang von Goethe, and Johannes Itten. The works of these individuals, in the 17th, 18th, and 20th centuries respectively, provide the foundations on which much of our understanding of color lies.

All three theorists explained colors in relation to a color wheel, using red, yellow, and blue as the primary colors. The color wheel is a simple but effective diagram developed to present the concepts and terminology of color theory. The traditional artists' wheel is a circle divided into 12 slices, as the image below indicates. Each slice is either a primary color, a secondary color, or a tertiary color.

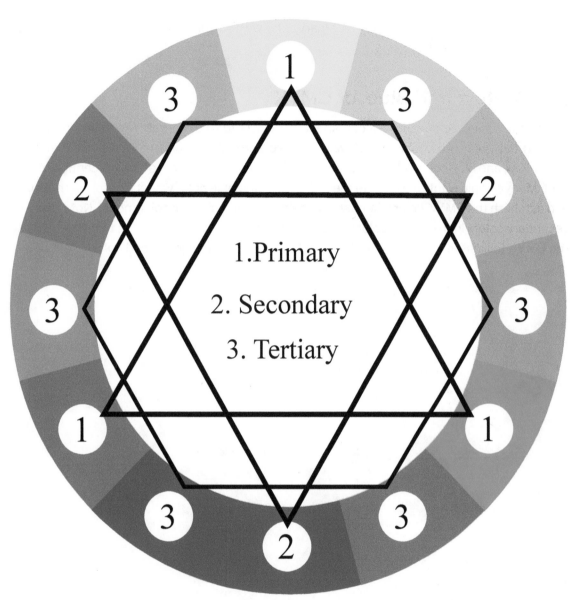

2-14. The traditional red, yellow, and blue artists' color wheel

**Primary colors**   The primary colors of the traditional color wheel are red, yellow, and blue. These hues form an equilateral triangle on the color wheel, and commencing from a primary color, every fourth color represents another primary color.

**Secondary colors**   By mixing two primary colors, we create secondary colors, indicated here by the small gray triangles. The secondary colors are orange, green, and purple.

**Tertiary colors**   There's a total of six tertiary colors: vermilion (red-orange), marigold (yellow-orange), chartreuse (yellow-green), aquamarine (blue-green), violet (blue-purple), and magenta (red-purple). As you might already have guessed, mixing a primary color with an adjacent secondary color forms a tertiary color.

## Red, Yellow, and Blue, or CMYK

I'm constantly amazed by the lack of respect that exists for the red, yellow, and blue primary color wheel. I've heard people call it invalid, archaic, and a kindergarten tool. It's true that the red, yellow, and blue color wheel is not a scientifically accurate model of the perception of light. Many people want to eliminate the red, yellow, and blue color wheel from art curricula, and establish the CMYK color wheel, shown below, as the universal color model. Note that the secondary colors in the CMYK color wheel are red, green, and blue, meaning that we could use the CMYK to illustrate both additive (using light) and subtractive (on paper) color.

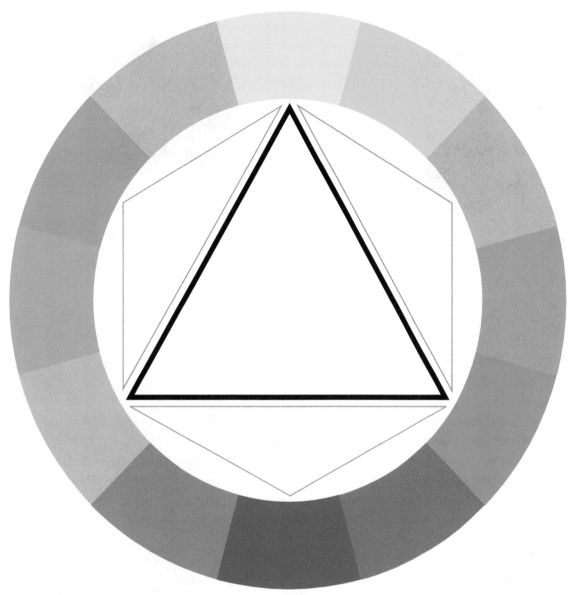

2-15. The CMYK color wheel

To illustrate the reasoning behind the push to move to CMYK, I've used gouache paints, which are basically watercolors that come in a tube. When mixed with water, they're fairly translucent and produce the colors you'd expect to see on the modern CMYK color wheel, as the figure below shows. Magenta and yellow mix to produce nice shades of orangey reds, while cyan and yellow mix to produce green and minty tones. This is how CMYK printing works. The inks are translucent and the overlap between them (along with the use of black) gives us most of the colors we can see on an additive, light-emitting monitor or TV. As the famous TV painting instructor Bob Ross might have said, "That's a happy little color model."

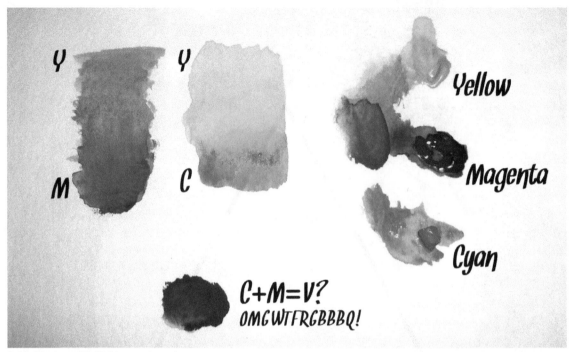

2-16. Playing with CMY gouache paints

Hang on a minute! What's that purple splodge? Yes, equal amounts of cyan and magenta form a violet or purple, instead of the pure blue suggested by the CMYK color wheel. In actuality, several anomalies like this crop up when we mix opaque pigments. The problem is that, if your paint is so thick that you're unable to see the white paper or canvas on which you're painting, the concept of a CMYK color wheel starts to fail. In this regard, the traditional red, yellow, and blue color wheel developed by Goethe, Itten, and others over the last four centuries or so is a superior model.

But we're using pixels, not paint! The reason many digital artists still keep a red, yellow, and blue color wheel handy is because the color schemes and concepts of traditional color theory are based on that model. As we'll see shortly, the relationships between colors are largely determined by their relative positions on the color wheel. But these positions differ depending on the wheel used. For instance, on the traditional color wheel, red and green are opposite one another, but on the CMYK wheel, cyan is opposite red. We can't simply shift the red and blue around the color wheel and call it a day.

Indeed, there are flaws to be found in both color wheel models. Complementary colors are a prime example. But the crowning head scratcher is that neither color wheel can fully describe the complexities of how we perceive color from light. Even though I design mostly for the Web—a medium that's displayed in RGB—I still use red, yellow, and blue as the basis for my color selections. I believe that color combinations created using the red, yellow, and blue color wheel are more aesthetically pleasing, and that good design is about aesthetics. For this reason, I'm going to present color theory as I learned it in my sophomore design fundamentals class in college—from the traditional red, yellow, and blue color wheel.

## The Scheme of Things

Currently, we know enough about colors to talk about their values, intensities, psychological associations, temperatures, and locations on the traditional color wheel. That's all well and good, but how do we find multiple colors that work together? This is where color schemes come in handy. **Color schemes** are the basic formulae for creating harmonious and effective color combinations. Six classic color schemes exist:

- monochromatic
- analogous
- complementary
- split complementary
- triadic
- tetradic (also called double complementary)

In order to employ any of these classic color schemes, we must start with a color. Consider the subject of the website you're working on, and choose a base color that suits the site's purpose. Of course, this choice may be out of your hands. Sometimes, you'll have to work within a company's rules, perhaps adhering to seemingly inane and eccentric color guidelines. But let's assume that the site you're designing is for a proud family of hoity-toity circus monkeys. These circus monkeys still believe they have a royal lineage, so they've requested that we incorporate a regal purple into the design. Silly monkeys … but you know what they say: "the client is always right."

### A Monochromatic Color Scheme

When we talked about the value of color earlier, we talked about tints and shades. A monochromatic color scheme—like the one below—consists of a single base color and any number of tints or shades of that color.

2-17. A monochromatic monkey

## Monochromatic Color Scheme in the Real World

Jewelry designer Amanda Braga[3] provides us with a killer example of monochromatic schemes. *Technically*, her site begins with a duotone panel, but then almost imperceptibly transitions between four different monochromatic themes as you scroll. The result is that the site feels rich and colorful as a whole, yet each section feels simple and cohesive. That's a clever trick to pull off.

---

3. http://www.amandabraga.com/

2-18. Amanda Braga employs multiple monochromatic schemes in her site

⬤ #000000   ⬤ #C72516   ⬤ #C7460F   ⚪ #E8B298

The site for <u>Frank Nitti Barbers</u>[4] features a special breed of *monochromaticism*. And, yes, I just made that word up. Any set of tones that consists solely of black, white, and shades of gray is known as an **achromatic** color scheme. The word achromatic literally means "without color." But just because the general scheme of the site has no color, it doesn't mean the content has to be colorless as well. A restrained use of gold gives Frank Nitti's dark "euro film noir" backdrop an important dose of warmth and richness.

[4] http://www.nittibarbers.sk/bratislava.html

2-19. Euro-cool "monochromaticism" at Frank Nitti Barbers

 #060606    #F0F0F0    #FFFFFF    #CDB585

2-20. Best Horror Scenes' creepy but neat monochromatic scheme

 #3e3e3e     #D74238     #E85D53        #F0F0F0

In the image above, <u>Best Horror Scenes</u>[5] mixes grungy, newspaper halftone effects with rich, blood-red tones to create a creepily neat and ordered feel.

---

[5]. https://besthorrorscenes.com/"

## An Analogous Color Scheme

2-21. An Analogous monkey

An **analogous color scheme** consists of colors that are adjacent to one another on the color wheel. If our color wheel were a delicious pie (mmm, pie!), then an analogous color scheme would be a fairly large slice. The key to creating a good analogous scheme is to remember that your eyes are bigger than your appetite. As a rule of thumb, avoid having a slice that's bigger than one third of the whole, or you're bound to make users sick.

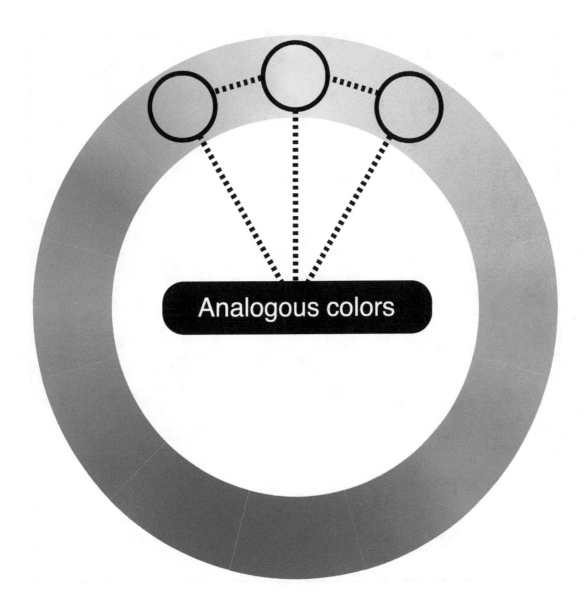

2-22. Analogous colors

## Analogous Color Scheme Examples

<u>The Portfolio of French animator Sandy Dauneau</u>[6] shows off her sublime motion skills with a deluge of electric blue and bubblegum pink. In fact, this site is a series of horizontal panels, each with a different analogous color scheme.

---

[6.] https://sandydauneau.fr/

2-23. French animator Sandy Dauneau's Portfolio site

ESPN launched a <u>minisite</u>[7] chronicling the evolution of basketball that takes a bold, playful approach to color. Each two-color panel stretches the idea of analogous colors to breaking point: these are one-third pie slices, yet they manage to pull it off by using slick composition and lots of space.

---

7. http://www.espn.com/espn/feature/story/_/id/24504198/

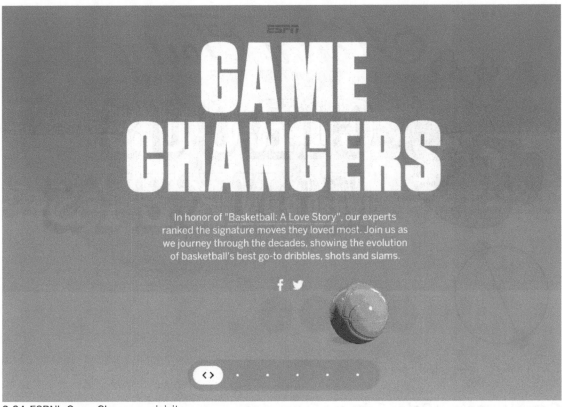

2-24. ESPN's Game Changers minisite

#FF8838      #39A4D6      #BE632B

## A Complementary Color Scheme

**Complementary color schemes** like the one featured in our updated hoity-toity illustration—shown below—consist of colors that are located opposite each other on the color wheel. Placing red-violet and yellow-green together is uncommon, but the monkeys insisted I keep some of their royal purple in the picture. Sheesh ... these clients are a bunch of primates.

2-25. A funky complementary monkey

## Complementary Color Scheme Examples

TelMD[8] is a health management app that makes broad use of a vibrant blue violet throughout its branding. However, you'll notice that all of its most important call-to-action buttons are rendered in an eye-catchingly complementary golden-yellow.

---

8. https://telmd.com/

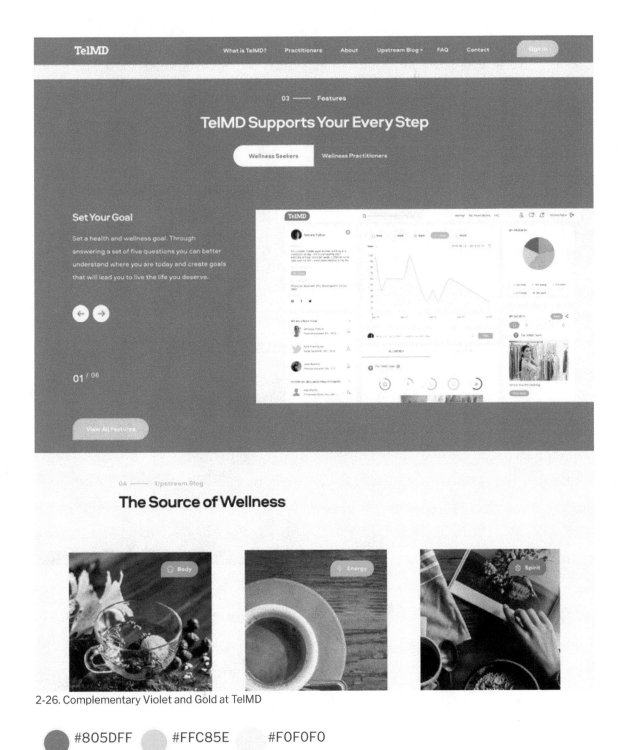

2-26. Complementary Violet and Gold at TelMD

⬤ #805DFF  ◯ #FFC85E  ◯ #F0F0F0

Dutch "unbreaking news" service The Correspondent[9] proves that complementary colors don't *have* to fight like spoiled kids for attention. Although the blue and red tones used here

9. https://thecorrespondent.com/

are very close to complementary, they've defused any clash by simply watering down the background blue. Interestingly, the Dutch language version of this site keeps the red but switches the pale blue for an equally pale green (notice the phone in the image below).

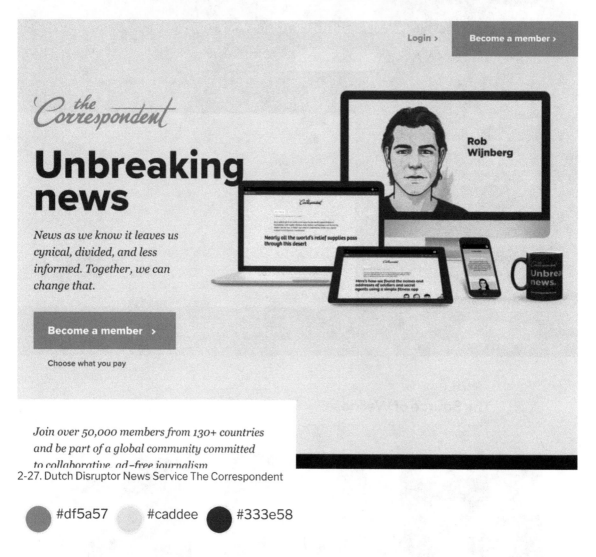

2-27. Dutch Disruptor News Service The Correspondent

⬤ #df5a57     ⬤ #caddee     ⬤ #333e58

It would be reasonable to guess that an organization called "Team Elite Kickboxing"[10] (or "Tek") wouldn't shy away from the idea of a "clash", and that comes through clearly in their color selections (overleaf). They positively embrace conflict and it *really* works!

Interestingly, the hues selected aren't very different from those used on the *The Correspondent* example. However, Tek's designers are happy to dial up the saturation and get right up in your face while they're at it. The rich duotone video loops are punchy and every design decision is strong yet cooly calculated. Anybody seeing a metaphor here? I really like

---

[10]. https://teamelitekickboxing.org/

the thinking behind this design.

2-28. Deep plum reds wrestle with deep navy blue in the Team Elite Kickboxing design

 #f54f54     #201E6B

## Common Complementary Pitfalls

Since complementary colors are so different from each other in many ways, they can cause an effect known as **simultaneous contrast** when placed together—each color making the other appear more vibrant and dominant. This is actually what makes complementary color schemes so successful at moving visitors' eyes around a composition. However, it can be horribly painful when complementary colors are used in a foreground–background relationship, as they are in the figure below. The lettering almost seems to hover uncomfortably above the backdrop.

#DE9746

#00BCF3

2-29. Beware! Sometimes nice colors don't play well together!

Another common pitfall is to choose colors that aren't directly opposite one another on the color wheel, yet aren't close enough to be analogous colors. These combinations are known as **discordants** because the colors will often clash with one another, causing viewer discord. In fact, 1980s fashion was all about discordant colors. Seeing a discordant color scheme these days tends to bring back fond memories of that geometric "designer series" of Trapper Keeper binders I loved so dearly at school. One of them is depicted below.

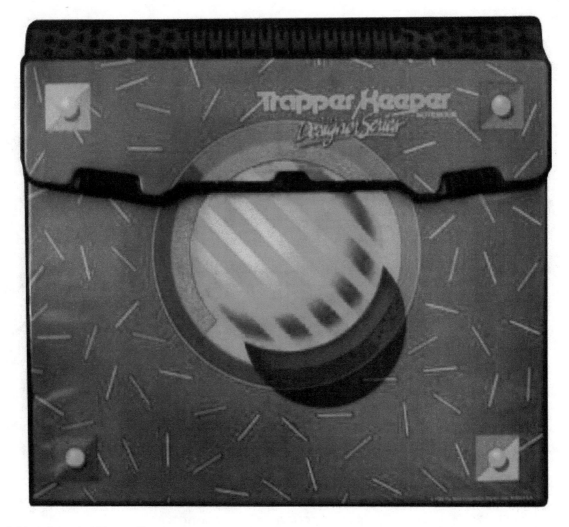

2-30. A discordant Trapper Keeper cover

As this example shows, this pitfall can be made workable if it's used intentionally. Discordant colors are whizzbang combinations that really appeal to children, teens, and tweens, so using them for youth-oriented sites or products is worth considering. They can also be used sparingly in more grown-up designs to create greater emphasis than can be achieved with just a simple complementary combination.

For an example of this type of color scheme, check out the Whole Festival[11] design below. Whole Festival's philosophy is defiantly nonconformist, and that idea is front and center in their design. Not only is the color palette discordant, but it changes literally every four seconds. What's more, key design components wander randomly around the screen while your cursor becomes a weird snake. This is an edge case, but if you're *trying* to unsettle

---

11. https://wholefestival.com/

people, here's the blueprint.

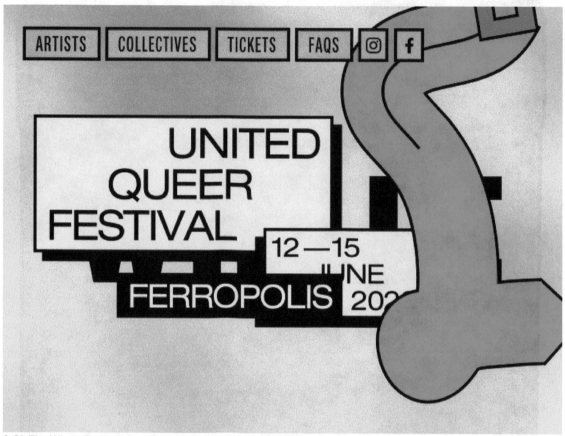

2-31. The Whole Festival site using peach, fluorescent pink, red, and mint-cream scheme.

#FFDC78     #FF41C3     #CBFDED     #FF0000

## Split-complementary, Triadic, and Tetradic

Split-complementary, triadic, and tetradic color schemes sound technical, but they're just simple variations of a basic complementary color scheme.

To create a **split-complementary** color scheme, use the two colors adjacent to your base color's complement. For example, take the left-most color scheme shown below. Red is the base color here, so instead of using green to form a complementary scheme, we'll use the two colors adjacent to green—chartreuse (yellow-green) and aquamarine (blue-green)—to form a three-color, split-complementary scheme. Note that, since you're using your base color with two discordant colors, this type of color scheme can look juvenile and extreme, but that may be just the effect you want.

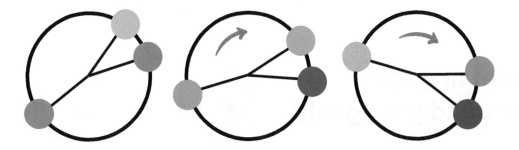

2-32. Split-complementary color scheme examples

For a **triadic** color scheme, we just push our split-complements out one more notch on each side, so that all the colors are equally spaced on the color wheel. Starting with red as our base color again, we select yellow rather than chartreuse, and instead of aquamarine, we select blue. This divides the color wheel into thirds; hence the *tri* prefix in triadic. In this example, which is the left-most scheme shown below, we have the three primaries (red, yellow, and blue) making up our color scheme. If you turned the scheme clockwise one notch, you'd have chartreuse (yellow-green), violet (blue-purple), and vermilion (red-orange), as shown in the middle example below.

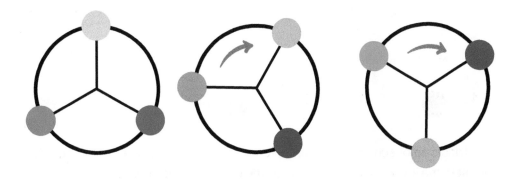

2-33. Triadic color scheme examples

Project management app Qoals[12] proves you can use color theory as a base but still change things up. They begin with a classic gold, green and purple triadic colorset, but also throw in a gold-complementing blue and a random magenta for good measure. The design feels fresh and fun but not messy.

---

[12.] http://qoals.com/

**qoals**

# Get aligned around your goals

Let's get rid of all boards, lists, deadlines, calendars...
Get aligned around what really matter the most.

Join the beta

### Set goals

Set and prioritize your
goals and let your team
know what matter the
most.

### Add tasks

Add and assign tasks to
define a clear roadmap
leading to your goal.

### Collect things

Collect resources related
to your goal in a single
place, accessible to
everyone.

### Track progress

See how things are
evolving at a glance and
stop asking everyone how
they are doing.

2-34. Qoals takes a measured approach to color

 #F5C432    #7756A6    #579DDC    #52D98D

Knowing that triadic color schemes involve three colors, you have probably deduced that a tetradic color scheme involves four colors. **Tetradic** color schemes combine any complementary color scheme with another complementary color scheme. The left-most example in the image below is a tetradic color scheme that combines orange and blue with yellow and purple.

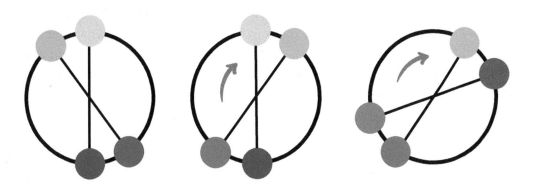

2-35. Tetradic color scheme examples

<u>Superlab.co</u>[13] combines simple primary shapes and some tasty animations with a tweaked tetradic scheme to great effect. The yellow and purple are complementary colors, as are the red and green. The designers throw in an extra darker purple ( *#36083C* ) to give it some extra depth and weight.

# Innovation through design.

We shape and design digital ideas and bring wonderful experiences to life.

2-36. Superlab using a tweaked tetradic color scheme

⬤ #FDC303   ⬤ #5D1E64   ⬤ #EC4137   ⬤ #6FDA9B

## Other Variants

Although most designers are aware of the standard color schemes, the combinations can

---

13. https://www.superlab.co/

tend to feel basic and uninspired. However, if you treat the color wheel like a dartboard, and pick whatever colors you land on, you're likely to come up with some truly awful combinations. (Trust me, I've tried it.) Rather than taking that risk, there are other ways to tweak the classic color schemes to create fresh combinations. Once you have a handle on monochromatic, analogous, and complementary color relationships, try experimenting with some of the following:

| | |
|---|---|
| **Monochromatic with mo' pop** | Rather than just using tints and shades of your base color, try incorporating pure gray, black, and white. This will create more contrast, and more "pop" within a monochromatic color scheme. |
| **Analo-adjust** | Adjust the saturation of one of the colors in your monochromatic scheme up and adjust the others down. A highly saturated color will stand out when placed among muted colors. |
| **Mono-split-complement** | If you have a good thing going with a split-complement color scheme but want to add some depth, try using a few tints and shades of your base color in the design. |

Obviously, I just made those names up, but you'll notice that all three variants are similar to the main traditional schemes. It's easy to tweak the traditional color schemes a little for more character, but remember that the color scheme you choose is the foundation upon which you'll build your website's color palette. And without a firm foundation, the rest of your design could come tumbling down.

# Creating a Palette

"A palette?" you might ask. "Isn't that the same as a color scheme?" Well, yes and no. A color scheme will only give you two, three, or four colors to work with. Although a limited palette can be beautiful, you're probably going to need a few more colors to design your website. It's better to nail down this process while you're thinking in the language of color, rather than pick ancillary colors at random as you need them for your layout. The number of colors you'll need will depend on the complexity of your design. I like to start off with at least five or six solid color choices before I even think about applying them to my layout.

## Hexadecimal Notation

Since this is the stage at which we become specific about each color we're choosing, we're going to need a standard way to refer to the colors in our palette. You probably already know about hexadecimal RGB color values, but if you don't, here's the quick drive-through version of the theory.

The hexadecimal counting system is much like the decimal counting system you're used to, except that instead of being based on multiples of ten, it's based on multiples of sixteen, and has six additional digits: *A* (which is the equivalent of decimal 10), *B* (11), *C* (12), *D* (13), *E* (14), and *F* (15).

So, what does this have to do with color palettes? Earlier in the chapter, I explained that your monitor uses an additive RGB color model, and that every pixel in the screen is "painted" using a combination of red, green, and blue light. What I didn't mention was that there are 256 different levels of red light, 256 levels of green light, and 256 levels of blue light. We can use these to create 16,777,216 distinct colors.

Thankfully, we have a way of describing each of these colors quickly and easily—by using hexadecimal color codes. A **hexadecimal** color code specifies the levels of red, green, and blue that go into a given color. For example, combining red, green, and blue at their highest possible values makes white. To use white in a web page, we set its red component to 255 ( `FF` in hexadecimal), its green component to 255 ( `FF` ), and its blue component to 255 ( `FF` ). We then combine these hexadecimal values in the order red, green, and blue and come up with the code `FFFFFF` .

Black, which is made by setting red, green, and blue to zero (00), has the code `000000` . Red, which we can create by setting red to `FF` and leaving green and blue at `00` , has the code `FF0000` . The figure below shows several standard colors with their hex value. After you've seen and used a lot of hex colors, you'll start to see the colors in the code. `#F26382` , for instance, is a coral-colored shade of pink, and `#371324` is the color of a slightly purple red wine. Once you think you've reached that Jedi Hex-Master status, head over to Yizzle.com,[14] for a little game of "What the Hex?"

| #660000 | #663300 | #003300 | #003399 | #330066 |
| #990000 | #993300 | #006600 | #0066ff | #660066 |
| #ff0000 | #ff3300 | #00ff00 | #00ccff | #990066 |
| #ff6666 | #ff6633 | #99ff99 | #99ccff | #ff6699 |

2-37. Hexadecimal color examples

## Color Tools and Resources

We now have a basic understanding of how colors are represented as hexadecimal values. The next step is to find out those values for each color we want to work with. Many resources are available to help you choose colors for your palette, including a ton of stand-alone applications and plugins for both Macs and PCs. We'll next look at a few of the favorites.

---

[14.] http://yizzle.com/whatthehex/

## Paletton

Although there are many online color pickers out there, my overall favorite is <u>Paletton</u>[15] (formerly known as Color Scheme Designer), shown below. Where many other applications use an RGB or CMYK color wheel, this awesome HTML tool uses the traditional red, yellow, and blue color wheel. Paletton visually explains color models beautifully and then allows you to take control them.

Once you have a palette you like, you can use the Vision Simulation options (bottom right) to model how your colors might appear to users with various categories of color blindness. When you're satisfied, you can export your colors as HTML/CSS, XML, plain text, a Photoshop palette, or a GIMP palette.

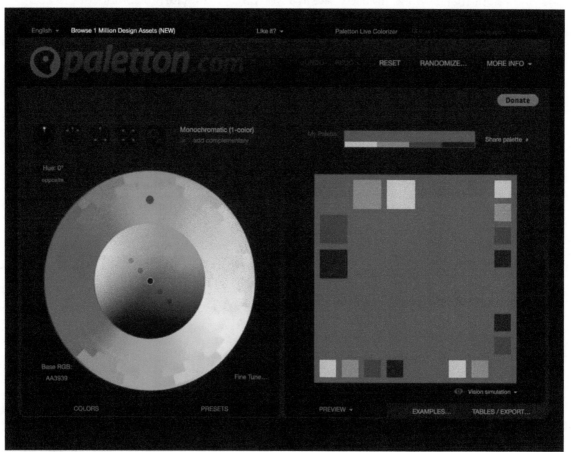

2-38. Paletton—the author's pick

---

15. http://paletton.com/

## Colormind

Colormind.io[16] gives the concept of a palette generator a nice spin—allowing you to instantly test-drive your new palette on a generic site template the site provides. Though that template is unlikely to match your application closely, it does give you a useful sense of how your colors work in a larger layout.

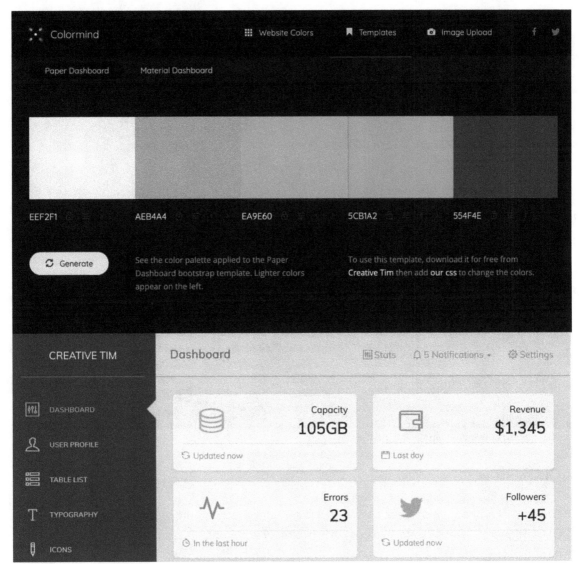

2-39. Colormind.io lets you instantly test-drive your palette

## Adobe Color

Originally launched as "Adobe Kuler" at a time when it was still super-hip to misspell your

---

16. http://colormind.io/template/

brand, <u>Adobe Color</u>[17] is still an excellent color selection resource. Color lets you create and save color combinations based on the standard color scheme configuration, not unlike the way Palleton works. Color will also generate a palette from any image you provide, as well as the option of stock imagery matched to your palette. Another key benefit of Color is the built-in Adobe community, allowing you to share and swap your color palettes with other users, and anyone can browse the most recent and highest-rated color combinations on the site.

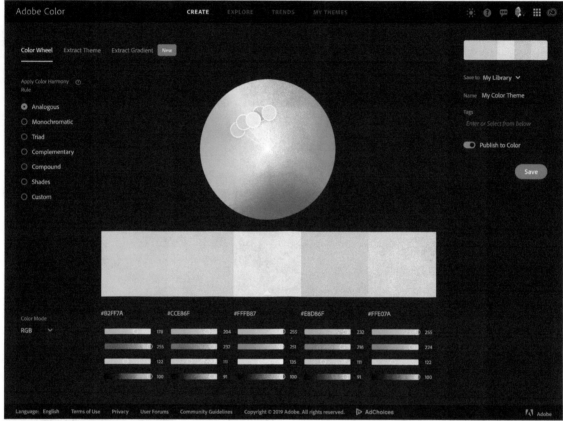

2-40. The now conventionally spelled "Adobe Color

## COLOURlovers

If the idea of sharing color resources with a like-minded community appeals to you, the <u>COLOURlovers</u>[18] website (shown below) is probably your jam. It's less of a color generator tool and more of an inspiration-sharing website. Though it began with just color schemes, you can now share patterns, shapes, templates and view color (or *colour*, if you insist) inspirations for a variety of design fields.

---

17. https://color.adobe.com/create/color-wheel
18. http://www.colourlovers.com/

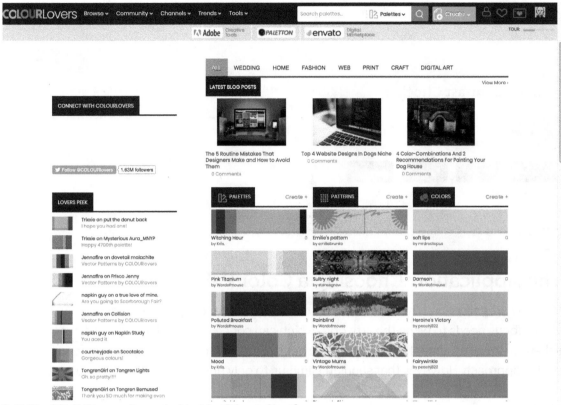

2-41. The COLOURlovers site: no doubt a labor/labour of love?

## Colour Contrast Checker

When choosing the colors for your palettes, it's essential to pick at least two colors that have enough contrast to be used as background and text colors. Some of the tools above will help you make good color decisions from the start.

But how do you know what "appropriate contrast" is?

The W3C's Web Content Accessibility Guidelines (WCAG 2.1https://www.w3.org/WAI/WCAG21/Techniques/general/G183") have determined that a contrast ratio is 4.5:1 for most body text and 3:1 for larger text provides enough contrast for the majority of users. There's a handful of tools that will help you calculate those ratios.

Personally I prefer to use a browser extensions for this task. Alex Clapperton's Colour Contrast Checker[19] is a nice point-n-click solution for Chrome, with sliders that let you tweak a color until you get a "pass tick".

---

[19.] https://chrome.google.com/webstore/detail/colour-contrast-checker/

2-42. Chrome Colour Contrast Checker extension, courtesy of Alex Clapperton of Colourcontrast.cc

## The Application: Choosing a Color Palette

Visit any art gallery and there's an obvious common theme to their interior design. As the visitor focus needs to be on the artwork—which can conceivably include any and every color scheme—galleries almost always choose a neutral color palette. We're going to need to take a similar approach. However, that shouldn't limit us to only pure shades of black and white.

The brand comes with a color—a maroon ( *#BA296F* )—so let's reuse that as highlight color. We could anticipate needing a hover/active state of that color and a general default text color too.

**Collecting Your Project Colors into CSS Variables**

Sometimes you'll select a color palette at the beginning of a project but later need to make adjustments. It's much easier if you can make any changes at a single point instead of having to search through CSS files for every occurrence of each color. In the past, your only option was to use a CSS preprocessor like Sass, Less or Stylus. These are still fine options, but today standard CSS lets us declare variables we can use across the site. Your variable name must begin with two dashes, and you should name it after *what it does*, not its current color. It will be confusing if the variable called `--red-button` has to be changed to blue later.

It makes sense to declare your variables at the very start of your CSS. In this example, we've created a CSS variable called `--color-highlight` and given it the color `#2F3E46`.

```
:root{
    --color-highlight: #2F3E46;
}
```

Now we can then use that color anywhere in our CSS by calling it like this:

```
.nav-item{
    color: var(--color-highlight);
}
```

If we ever need to update that color, we'll only need to edit the CSS in one place.

I want to break up the layout by using a mix of light and dark panels, so I'll need a selection of tones. If I wanted a completely neutral set, I might set up a stepped palette like this:

#F2F2F2    #B2B2B2    #7C7C7C    #4F4F4F    #3E3E3E

On a standard color-picker, all of these grays would sit along the far left edge of the colorspace, meaning they contain equal amounts of red, green and blue. This gives us a functional set of tones, but there's also something a little artificial and lifeless about it. In fact, perfectly neutral grays are very rare in the real world. Take a close look at the color choices in the work of these old masters (below) and you'll notice that their grays always pick up color from their surroundings.

2-43. Three shades of gray: The Creation Of Adam, by Michelangelo; Napoleon Crossing The Alps, by Jacques-Louis David; and Olympia, by Edouard Manet

What happens if we take out neutral grays and push those color-picker markers just a little to right?

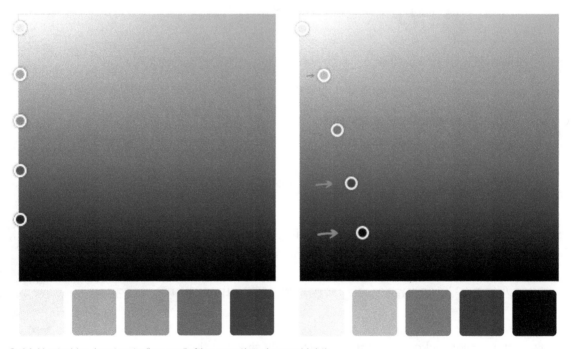

2-44. Neutral (or desaturated) grays (left) versus tinted grays (right)

In the example above, the neutral grays (left) appear thin and clinical beside richer "green-grays" on the right. If we'd pushed the color-pickers further to the right, the palette would become bonafide greens, but we've managed to keep them as "gray tones with a greenish twist".

 #F2F2F2     #AFC6C     #808E8B     #4E5A57    ● #242C2A

I like that. It should be neutral enough to work with any artwork, but not too cold or antiseptic.

There are two important points to make here:

1   There's nothing special about the green we used as the tint. Adding controlled amounts of *any* color to gray will give it life.

2   Be mindful that lighter grays get overwhelmed by a tint much more easily than dark grays do, which is why my darker color-picker markers get progressively further to the right. It's the same reason it takes less food dye to color water than Coke.

Finally, if I were building an HTML prototype, I would add these colors as CSS variables to the top of my CSS:

```
--color-branding:       #BA296F;
--color-branding-hover: #FF0C80;
--color-text:           #222222;

/* grays*/
--color-fill-1:         #F2F2F2;
--color-fill-2:         #AFC6C0;
--color-fill-3:         #808E8B;
--color-fill-4:         #4E5A57;
--color-fill-5:         #242C2A;
```

Being able to come up with a unique color palette is all about keeping your eyes open. If you see a website, advertisement, illustration, or other graphic that stands out, try to figure out what the dominant colors are, and what type of color scheme underlies the palette. Remember, though, that color inspiration can come from anywhere. Is there a color that reminds you of a certain song? How about the colors of your favorite meal? Maybe there's even a color in that tacky seventies wallpaper in your parents' house that would work well for you. Being aware of the kinds of issues associated with color usage will give you an eye for color and an ability to come up with original palettes that fulfill the requirements of your client.

With the color choices made, it's time to consider adding depth to the site. Flat design has been the default for most of the last decade, but there are other options to consider. The right texture can add a lot to a design, but it has to fit with the concept and overall direction of the site. This is what we'll discuss in the next chapter.

# Texture

There are many well-intentioned designers out there who build a standard two- or three-column website layout, pick a few colors for it, and call it a day. They don't bother pushing their design any further, or tweaking any details. Perhaps there's no time or money in the project budget to go the extra distance, or maybe they've taken the "less is more" axiom a little too literally. Not every website has to be beautiful, but every website can be. CSS has given web designers a great amount of control over how a site looks, but I think the real problem is that many people are just unsure where to start when it comes to customization. This chapter is all about that process: taking your design a step further with the help of texture.

**Texture** is anything that gives a distinctive appearance or feel to the surface of a design or object. When you put your hands on a brick wall, a wooden beam, or a wet bar of soap, what do you feel? Can you make a website "feel" like one of these surfaces? Thankfully, it's impossible for a website to give visitors splinters, but you *can* make it relate to and evoke memories of real materials. First, you need a way to describe the surface. You might start off by talking about relative roughness or smoothness, but there are other factors that give a surface its unique characteristics. Does the texture incorporate repeated patterns? Does it have a unique shape? What are the lines like that make up the shape? Does the shape have volume?

These questions might seem random, but they arise directly from the elements of graphic design: point, line, shape, volume and depth, and pattern. Understanding these components will help you not only to explain texture, but to create it as well.

# Point

If you've worked with CSS, then you're probably familiar with using pixels as a unit of measurement. One pixel (short for "picture element") is one of the millions of dots on your computer screen. If your resolution is set to 1280×1024 pixels, you have 1,310,720 pixels on your screen, arranged in 1,024 rows and 1,280 columns. All these pixels come together to create a digital image.

This is all very elementary technical knowledge, but as we're about to see, it applies specifically to the concept of points in graphic design.

Just as the pixel is the fundamental element of digital images, the **point** (or dot) is the fundamental element of graphic design, and can be used to build any graphic element. Points have no scale or dimension unless they have a frame of reference. For instance, a point on a huge billboard might look like a period, but up close it's probably about as big as your head. When points are grouped together, as they are in the figure below, they can create lines, shapes, and volume.

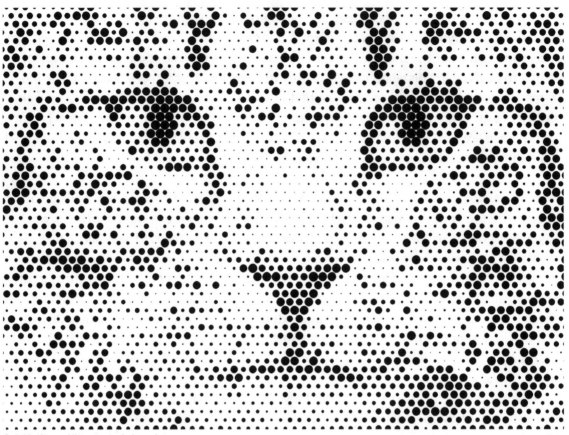

3-1. Halftone Kitty: a study in points

When you're working on website graphics, it's easy to look at the big picture and ignore the points that make up each image. Points themselves have a lot of power, though. Just take a look at Craig Robinson's <u>Flip Flop Flyin'</u>[1]. Among other forms of tiny art, Craig creates portraits of famous people, bands, and groups that he calls Minipops. The one below is a close-up of Craig's A-Team Minipop. Hard-core fans will notice that Hannibal even has his trusty cigar.

---

[1] http://flipflopflyin.com/

3-2. The A-Team, by Craig Robinson

# Line

When two or more points are connected, they form a line. The line is the most common element of graphic design, and is among the most expressive. When designing websites, most people only consider lines for CSS borders or hyperlink underlines, but they can be used in countless ways throughout your web creations.

When a line is diagonal, it evokes a sense of movement and excitement. Like a falling domino, a diagonal line has potential energy. Using a pattern of horizontal lines as a background element provides texture and interest to a design, but using a motif of diagonal lines will make the design feel a little more "on edge," causing users' eyes to move around constantly. Compare the two examples below. Which keeps your eyes moving around more successfully?

### Horizontal

It's an important and popular fact that things are not always what they seem. For instance, on the planet Earth, man had always assumed that he was the most intelligent species occupying the planet, instead of the third most intelligent.

### Diagonal

It's an important and popular fact that things are not always what they seem. For instance, on the planet Earth, man had always assumed that he was the most intelligent species occupying the planet, instead of the third most intelligent.

3-3. Backgrounds created using diagonal and horizontal lines

Just as diagonal lines suggest movement, varying the thickness and direction of a line generates a sense of expression and character. Jagged lines with sharp angles can feel dangerous and frantic. Gently rolling, curvy lines tend to feel relaxing and smooth. Lines comprising 90-degree angles tend to feel sharp and mechanical. Finally, lines with lots of curves and angles convey expressiveness—such as handwriting, graffiti, and sketches.

When you're working on the prototype stage of a website's development, try to keep in mind that lines are far more useful than just being dividers, borders, and stripes. They're the foundation of art, drawing, and design. As the Web is such a rigid and technical medium, it's easy to forget about fundamental art tools such as pens and brushes. So try creating variations in the quality of a line, either by scanning in some of your own traditional artistic endeavors, or using the predefined brushes in a program like Adobe Illustrator, as I have below. This is a great way to bring a traditional artistic feel to a medium that's sometimes all too digital.

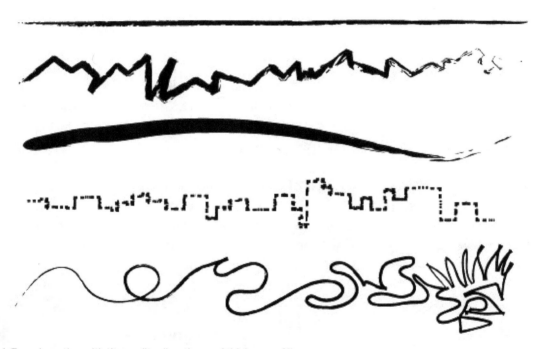

3-4. Experimenting with the quality, direction, and thickness of line

## Shape

Any time the two end points of a line come together, a **shape** is created. There's probably little more I can add to your knowledge of the basic geometric shapes—circles, triangles, and rectangles. Arrows, stars, diamonds, ellipses, plus signs, semicircles and more are geometric as well. The image below illustrates a few of them. The precise curves, angles, and straight lines involved in geometric shapes make them difficult to draw by hand, unless you have a compass, protractor, and ruler. On a computer, though, geometrically defined lines, curves, and angles are usually the default forms in any image-creating program. For that reason, these types of shapes have a reputation for feeling technical and mechanical.

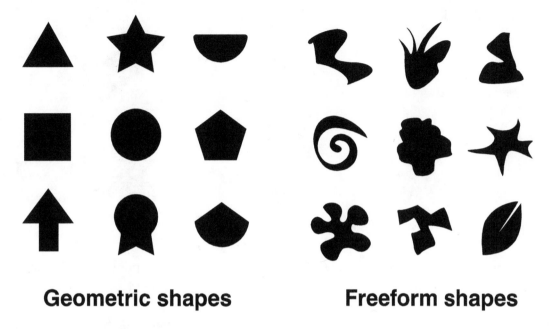

**Geometric shapes**          **Freeform shapes**

3-5. Geometric and freeform shapes

The other main category of shape is organic or freeform. **Freeform** shapes are more abstract than geometric shapes, and consist of non geometric curves, random angles, and irregular lines, as can be seen above. Freeform shapes have a free-flowing nature that conveys a sense of informality and spontaneity. They can represent the outline of a product, human gestures, or an organic doodle. The example below represents the gradual transformation of a geometric shape into a freeform shape.

3-6. Transforming a geometric shape into an organic one

When it comes to website design, it can be easy to forget that freeform shapes exist. In Chapter 1, I explained how the anatomy of a website consists of a bunch of blocks. No matter how you arrange them on the page, these blocks are inherently geometric. Unlike print design, which gives us the freedom to draw whichever layout shapes we like, the Web limits us to rectangles. However, although the containing blocks may be rectangular, that doesn't mean they have to *look* rectangular.

3-7. Organic layouts from Die Zeit and Rolling Stone

As these examples from _Die Zeit_[2] and _Rolling Stone_[3] magazine show, print layouts often reshape text blocks to help illustrate the story.

Modern browsers now allow you shape the flow of text using CSS Shapes. The simplest non-rectangular shape to apply to text is the circle. In the example below, we're floating the image of Neptune to the left of the text. Normally, we'd expect the text to form a vertical edge against the right edge of the Neptune image. However, if we apply a class with `shape-outside: circle(50%)` to the image, the text immediately wraps around an invisible circle inside the area of the image.

---

[2] https://www.zeit.de/

[3] https://www.rollingstone.com/

3-8. Applying shape-outside: circle(50%) to the planet image allows us to flow text around a circular shape

 **CodePen Demo**

You can see a CodePen demo of this technique at https://codepen.io/alexmwalker/pen/qBOwaWX

That 50% figure generates a circle radius half the width the image. Any parts of a `circle()` larger than the image get automatically cropped, leaving flat edges. At about 70% there will be no circle edge left visible. Circles smaller than 50% create a "shrinking island" that the text will flow into and around.

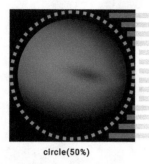
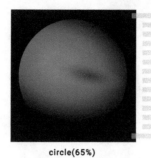
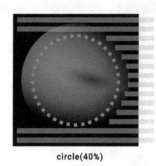

| circle(50%) | circle(65%) | circle(40%) |

3-9. Setting circle() to greater than 70% is redundant

But let's face it: there are only so many circular dinner plates, coins or planet layouts to wrap your text around. The ability to flow text around *any* shape is a much more powerful design tool, and this is exactly what the `shape-outside:polygon(…)` option allows you to do. Generate a set of polygon coordinates contoured to your image and you should be able to wrap text around practically any image.

In practical terms, I've found that creating a polygon shape can be tricky, as most SVG editors prefer to convert shapes into PATHs rather than POLYGONs. <u>BoxySVG</u>[4] is the one SVG editor I've found that *will* keep your polygons as polygons. <u>Bennett Freely's Clippy</u>[5] tool is another useful option for generating polygon coordinates:

```
/* Star shape */
shape-outside: polygon(50% 0%, 61% 35%, 98% 35%, 68% 57%,
    79% 91%, 50% 70%, 21% 91%, 32% 57%, 2% 35%, 39% 35%);
```

Ultimately, I've found the simplest way to shape text is to simply plug an SVG URL directly into the `shape-outside` property ( `shape-outside: url(arm.svg)` . In this working example, I'm going to riff on the classic Saul Bass movie poster for <u>*The Man with the Golden Arm*</u>[6].

---

[4.] https://boxy-svg.com/

[5.] https://bennettfeely.com/clippy/

[6.] https://en.wikipedia.org/wiki/The_Man_with_the_Golden_Arm

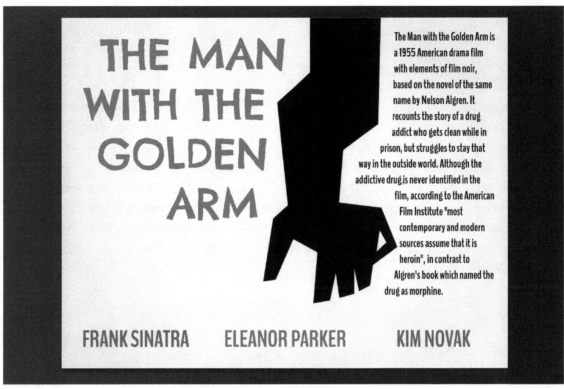

3-10. A tribute to a Saul Bass movie poster that wraps text around a roughly cut arm shape

I started by splitting the movie title and the description text into two separate column *div* s. The SVG arm graphic was then slotted in immediately before the movie title and floated to the right:

```
<div class="row-1">
    <div class="title">
      <img class="arm" src="arm.svg" alt="arm" />
      <h1>The Man with the Golden Arm</h1>
    </div>
    <div class="description">
      <p>...</p>
    </div>
  </div>
```

If we give the arm graphic a negative *margin-right* , we can make it straddle the right and left columns. Applying that same SVG graphic to *shape-outside* property of the image then instantly reshapes the text to fit the left edge of the arm:

```
img.arm {
  shape-outside: url(arm.svg);
  shape-margin: 15px;
```

```
    float: right;
    margin-top: 0px;
    margin-right: -100px;
}
```

Nice. However, since our description text (that is, the right column) lives in a different column from our SVG image, we'll need to be a little bit crafty to make the text wrap on the right side.

To tackle this, we'll need to create a new `:before` pseudo element inside the right-hand panel, give it the exact size of our SVG arm, and then load the SVG arm into the background. We now have two copies of the arm SVG on screen. However, if we use negative margins we can carefully reposition this new image to sit *precisely* on top of the original SVG image. Add the `shape-outside: url(arm.svg)` property and our description text immediately contours itself to our arm:

```
.description:before {
    display: block;
    position: relative;
    float: left;
    content: '';
    width: 200px;
    height: 400px;
    margin-left: -100px;
    margin-top: -1rem;
    background-image: url(arm.svg); /* delete: used for positioning only */
    shape-outside: url(arm.svg);
    shape-margin: 20px;
}
```

The nice thing is, once we have the text flow working, we can safely remove the background-image and just leave the `shape:outside` to do its job.

 **CodePen Demo**

> You can see a CodePen demo of this example at https://codepen.io/alexmwalker/pen/NWGZbGP

## Designing in CSS

Some designers have created amazing artwork without images, using pure CSS. The image below shows off the amazing animation work of Agathe Cocco[7]. Agathe took Tony Babel's

---

[7] https://codepen.io/agathaco

<u>artwork</u>[8], rebuilt it from a complex stack of HTML $div$ s, and then stitched a series of CSS animations into that HTML. You can see the <u>full example on CodePen</u>[9]. Other examples of pure CSS artwork include <u>Nicolas Gallagher's pure CSS GUI icons</u>[10].

3-11. An amazing CSS Box Dog animation created in pure CSS by the very talented Agathe Cocco

## Rotation and Angles

I mentioned at the start of this chapter that diagonal lines often evoke a sense of movement and excitement. Rotating elements "off the square" in your design can have a similar effect. Angled objects break up the horizontal and vertical monotony of the Web and create new paths that lead the eye into the design.

Wedding planners <u>Foudamour.ca</u>[11] (above) provide a good example. Their tasteful pastel tones and romantic photography are entirely orthodox, but simply angling the imagery injects so much extra energy into the layout. It also creates curling "whitespace tracks" that draw your eye down and around the layout.

---

8. ttps://dribbble.com/shots/4934623-Box-Doggie
9. https://codepen.io/agathaco/full/eLOKvr
10. http://nicolasgallagher.com/pure-css-gui-icons/demo/
11. https://www.foudamour.ca/

3-12. Wedding planners Foudamour.ca use angles to create a natural flow between focal points

The ability to guide people's eyes with text, imagery and whitespace is a big part of your success as a designer. This is an idea that applies as much to books, newspapers, and even movie posters as it does the Web. Let's see it in action in a classic movie poster.

## Directing the Eye

In most layouts, we have a list of page elements—such as headings, images, and text—and position them on the page. In the classic poster for the movie *Breakfast at Tiffany's* (below), you could argue there are three major focal points:

- Audrey Hepburn's face

- her billing credit text at the top right
- the *Breakfast at Tiffany's* movie title

Study it for longer and you might notice the cat and the kissing couple, but it's difficult *not* to be almost magnetically drawn back to her face. It turns out that humans are very good at noticing what other people are looking at. We're naturally nosey creatures and want to know what others find interesting.

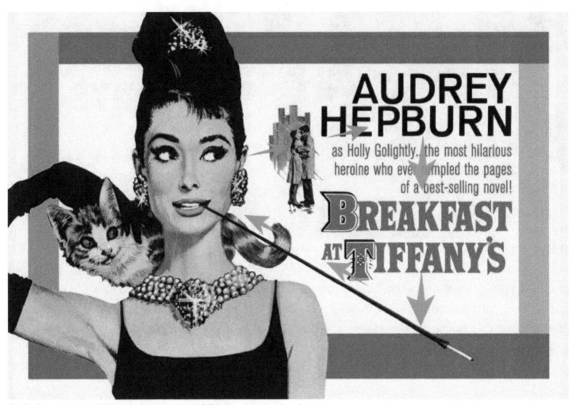

3-13. Breakfast at Tiffany's Poster: try NOT following Audrey's eyes

And where is Audrey looking? We almost can't help following her eyes, past the lovers, to her starring credit before naturally reading our way down to the movie title.

Then we hit that huge cigarette extender. Why did they decide to make it almost comically long? It's long because it creates a natural path that draws our eye *straight back* to the lovely Audrey—and we probably begin that loop again. Even the little cat's eyes help reinforce this circuit. It's as if an invisible tour guide is directing our attention through the layout.

But what happens if we make a tiny Photoshop edit and turn her glance back towards us? Let's try it in the image below.

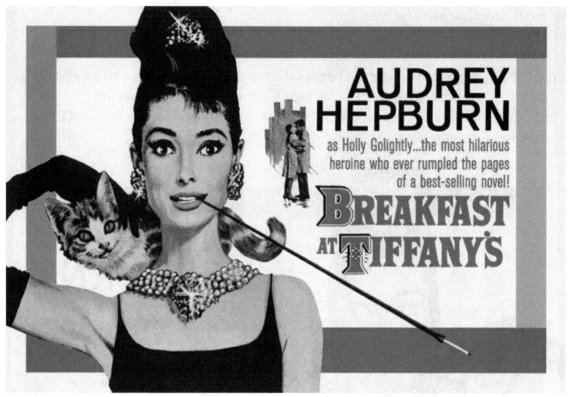

3-14. Audrey is looking at me! Who cares about that dumb text now?

Such a trivial change alters the flow of this poster dramatically. Audrey is no longer interested in that text, so it's instantly less interesting to us too. Sure, we can force ourselves towards the text, but our eye no longer glides effortlessly around the whole composition. Instead, it's almost like there's an invisible gravity pulling us back to Audrey. This can have a huge effect on how users interact with our interfaces.

## Putting It Into Practice

Great UI design is often about drawing attention to just the right thing at just the right time. I think this "eye line" technique is underutilized on the Web, but there are a few good examples out there. Although they've redesigned their site recently, I particularly loved the way t-shirt maker Real Thread[12] (Figure 3-15) previously used this idea.

---

12. https://www.realthread.com/

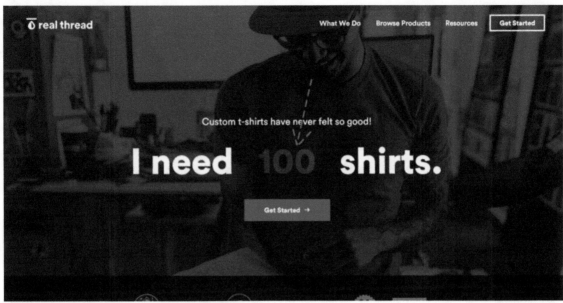

3-15. Real thread: where do they want us to look?

This Real Thread design takes a fantastically bold, no-nonsense sales approach. Rather than trying to sell you on the idea of buying t-shirts, it jumps the conversation straight to *"how many do you want?"* This page is 95% focused on accomplishing this singular task—getting you to enter a number to complete the sentence *"I need X shirts"*. In the background, we see a happy, tattooed, t-shirt–making hipster setting the scene. And where is this guy looking? Out at us? Around the room?

No, he's looking *directly* at the blinking cursor—reinforcing the only thing the company wants you to pay attention to. Super clever. This is a very simple layout, but I suspect it was a very effective page design.

Be aware: this "follow the eyeline" technique takes more work to implement, as you'll need to be planning for it from the start, rather than sourcing images towards the end of the project. You might get lucky and find just the right stock photo, but it's more likely that you'll need to take your own photos to get the eyeline angles you want. That shouldn't be a big deal, as most of us can source a decent camera at a pinch.

## Volume and Depth

We've talked about point, line, and shape, but now it's time to take this chapter to another dimension. The elements we've discussed so far only exist in two dimensions: width and height. They're just marks on paper or a screen, without any indication of depth. However, as we live in a world of three dimensions, we've learned to rely on visual cues that help us to determine the width, height, and depth of the objects around us.

## Perspective

When we see a path that disappears into the horizon, as the Great Wall of China does below, we don't think that its width actually decreases to a single point. Similarly, when we look at an open door, we're aware that the top and bottom of the door are parallel, even though they seem to converge towards the door frame. We're not fooled by these spatial illusions, because we know (consciously or otherwise) that objects tend to look smaller as they become further away.

3-16. Perspective on the Great Wall of China

## Proportion

In Chapter 1, I mentioned that altering the proportion of objects was a good way to create emphasis. This is true because we humans rely on the relative proportion of adjacent objects to determine not only the size of those objects, but also their location in three-dimensional space. Although the horses in the background of the image below are proportionately smaller than the horse in the foreground, our eyes tell us that they're about the same size in reality.

3-17. Proportion in design is more than just horseplay

## Light and Shadow

Light and shadow are the most important visual cues we can use to determine or create depth and volume in compositions. Even with accurate perspective and proportion, a composition without highlights and shadowing will look flat. Light and shadow establish visual contrast, and help to create the illusion of three-dimensional depth with two-dimensional media, such as pencil on paper or pixels on your computer screen. Light and shadow alone can also be used to make two-dimensional objects look like they exist in three-dimensional space.

Each of the three cyan-colored circles below are the same size, but the different lighting effects and shadows applied give each a unique feeling of depth and volume. A basic drop shadow has been applied to the first circle. It's obvious that this is a two-dimensional object, but the drop shadow gives the illusion that the circle is hovering above the surface beneath it. The second circle has a linear gradient, and a shadow that's skewed to the right. This combination of light with the tilted shadow suggest that it's a two-dimensional circle that's casting a shadow on an angled surface.

The fact that the shadow is closer to the bottom than the top of the circle creates a sense of movement: it looks as if the top of the circle is falling towards or away from the viewer's eye. A

**radial gradient**—meaning one that's applied in all directions from a central point—has been applied to the third circle, which looks spherical due to the highlight and shadows that the gradient creates. The shadow that it casts matches the location of the light source, which lends credibility to the volume and depth of the shape.

3-18. Examples of light and shadow

## From 3D Renders to Flat design

If you were around for the early versions of Apple's iOS, you might remember it had a unifying design idea: apps were richly rendered imitations of their real-world equivalents. For example:

- the podcast app looked like a reel-to-reel tape player
- the sound recorder was a shiny, metal microphone with brushed steel buttons
- the Find My Friends app had stitching and leather trim

This is a design approach called **skeuomorphism** and, to be fair, it wasn't a horrible idea at the time. The original iPhone was entirely different from all the phones before it, so the idea of making the sound recorder look like a microphone helped explain the new functionality to new users. As they say, "*Show, don't tell*".

3-19. Skeuomorphic design in the podcast app, sound recorder and Find My Friends app

However, there are some undeniable downsides to skeuomorphism.

1    Once you understand the purpose of an app, the real-world imagery becomes mostly
redundant. In the recorder screen example above (center), more than four fifths of the
interface is wasted on a picture.

2    Sometimes skeuomorphic design accidentally transmits bad information. For instance,
the reel-to-reel tapes in the iOS podcast app used to authentically stream tape from left to
right, giving you an idea of progress. Yet every podcast began with precisely the same amount
of tape, whether the podcast was two minutes in length or two hours. It echoed real-life, but
not.

3    Often these real-world analogs are becoming less and less relevant every day. How
many 20-year-olds have ever used a tape deck? A phone handset? A leather-bound
appointment book? Analogies are only useful if everyone knows them.

## Flat Design

Over the next five years, designers began to drift away from the finely rendered detail of
skeuomorphism towards a simpler, less decorative design style. It was actually Microsoft who

got the flat ball rolling with their Metro UI, and then successive versions of Android and IOS got flatter and visually simpler. Eventually, Material Design distilled it all down into a cohesive theory. **Flat design** stripped away all non-critical decoration, gradients, shadows and colors to give complete focus on the remaining UI elements.

And on the whole, we're all much better off for it. Graphics files are lighter and faster, and UIs are simpler and less cluttered.

3-20. Poster children for the Flat Design Movement, Clear App, Rechner and Gmail

Of course, there are some who might argue that flat design *can* have a cool, clinical sameness to it. So, where to from here?

## Is UI Design Still a Flat Earth?

Although the design pendulum is unlikely to swing all the way back to 3D photorealistic UIs, many designers have found ways to add some natural warmth and grain to flat designs without loading up on visual clutter. Print design can give us some useful clues here. In the first half of the 20th century, most print design was "flat design" simply because that was all most printing presses could produce.

Ironically, those same low-tech printing techniques often accidentally gave that work extra character. Check out the vintage labels shown below. You'll see the flat color designs showing rough paper grain, halftone dots, rough organic edges and ink bleeding together. We can steal this idea.

3-21. The imperfections of paper and printing often accidentally adds natural warmth and charm to a design

## Photoshop Filters

So, do I need to eBay a vintage printing press now? That could be fun, but no. Photoshop Plugin developers like Mr Retro have made a living out of riffing on old print styles with their Permanent Press[13] set of filters. Each filter mimics different aspects of the natural, grungy imperfections of offset presswork. These print glitches include:

- rough paper grains
- chunky halftone dots
- misaligned printing plates
- ink overlap and bleed

3-22. Before and after Mister Retro's Permanent Press Photoshop filters

These filters are highly configurable and can add a heap of tactile warmth to flat-color designs without necessarily adding a lot more clutter—especially if used sparingly. However, at $99 they aren't cheap. But there are other less expensive ways to squeeze some of the flatness out of a design. We'll cover some of them in this chapter.

## Pattern

I still remember my first exposure to website design. I was in a tenth-grade typing class and the instructor took it upon herself to teach us HTML. It was optional, but choosing between timed typing tests and learning how to build web pages was an easy choice to make. By the end of that year I'd created quite a few little websites. The common denominator among those admittedly hideous creations was repeating backgrounds. You probably know the kind

13. https://www.misterretro.com/filters/permanent-press

I'm talking about: those backgrounds that tile seamlessly to give the appearance of continuous water, stone, starry skies, metal, or canvas texture.

Although repetitious background images like the ones below are the hallmark of early 1990s web design, they're also classic examples of pattern. Pattern has long been used to add richness and visual interest to all types of design. On the Web, seamless background images were originally favored because they reduced page size and download times. Using a small image that could be tiled to fill a background area, rather than a large non-tiling image, significantly reduced the download time for website visitors with 56k modems.

3-23. Typical 1990s tiling website backgrounds

Just because tiling background images with repeated patterns has a tacky past, it doesn't mean you should avoid it today. In fact, it's used more often than you probably realize. CSS has greatly improved the degree of control designers have over the way background images work. Before CSS was around, we could only assign background images to *body* and *table* elements. Now, with CSS, backgrounds can be applied to just about any element you choose. You can use any of five CSS properties (and one additional shorthand property) to set the background of an element:

*background-color:*

This is the property we use to set a solid background color for any element. For example, if we wanted to set the background color of an element to a nice green-blue ( *#00B2CC* ), we'd add the following declaration to the element's style rule:

```
background-color: #00B2CC;
```

When using hexadecimal values in CSS, you need to prefix the color code with `#`, as shown above. You can also specify `transparent` here if you don't want the background of your element to be filled with a color. `transparent` is actually the default value of the `background-color` property. You might be tempted to use an HTML color name, like `Aquamarine` or `BlanchedAlmond`, but as only 16 color names are officially sanctioned by the W3C in the HTML 4.0 specification (and even those will generate warnings when you try to validate your CSS), it's recommended that you use the hexadecimal values we talked about in Chapter 2.

`background-image:`

If we want an image to be used as the background of an element, we can specify that image using the `background-image` property. The possible values for this property are `url("filename")` or `none`. If we wanted to set the background of an element to `animalcracker.png`, we'd add the following declaration to that element's style rule:

```
background-image: url("origami.png");
```

`background-repeat:`

There are four possible values for `background-repeat`: `repeat`, `repeat-x`, `repeat-y`, and `no-repeat`. The default value is `repeat`, which sees that the specified background image will be tiled vertically and horizontally. The `repeat-x` setting will cause the background image to be repeated horizontally. This is handy if you want to apply a horizontally tiling image or gradient to an element, but want the rest of that element to be filled with the specified background color. Similarly, `repeat-y` specifies that the background image should be repeated vertically. Finally, `no-repeat` is used when you have a background image that you don't want to tile at all. The effect of each of these settings is shown below.

background-repeat: repeat (default)    background-repeat: repeat-x    background-repeat: repeat-y    background-repeat: no-repeat

3-24. The effects of different background-repeat settings

*background-attachment*

This property determines whether the background image stays in the same location or moves with the content when the page is scrolled. It can be set to the values of *fixed* or *scroll*, the latter of which is the default. When *background-attachment* is set to *fixed*, the background will be fixed relative to the viewport (or browser window), so that when you scroll the page, the background image will stay in the same location.

*background-position:*

This property controls the position of a background image and accepts two values: the horizontal and vertical position of the image. These values can be set using CSS measurements, percentages, or keywords ( *right*, *center*, or *top* for the horizontal position; *top*, *center*, or *bottom* for the vertical). For example, if you wanted a background image to be centered horizontally and aligned to the top of an element, you could specify this using keywords ( *background-position: center top* ) or using percentages ( *background-position: 50% 0%* ). If we wanted to position the image 300 pixels from the left edge, and 400 pixels from the top, we could use the declaration *background-position: 300px 400px* . The effect of both of these possible values is shown below.

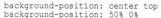

background-position: center top
background-position: 50% 0%          background-position: 300px 400px          background-position: 100% 100%

3-25. Origami birds with different background-position settings

*background-size:*

This property controls the scaling of the background image. By default, background images will render at their inherent pixel size. The *background-size* property will stretch or compress your background to the size you specify. It looks for two values—a width and a height, in that order. If only one value is provided, it will apply the same value to both. Valid values for *background-size* include *auto* , *(unit length/%)* , *cover* , *contain* , *initial* and *inherit* . *Cover* is the equivalent of *100% 100%* .

background-size: 100% auto        background-size: auto 100%        background-size: 50% auto

3-26. Various combinations of the CSS background-size property

To help streamline all this background code, the developers of CSS have created a **shorthand property**, which allows us to specify all six of these properties in a single background declaration. It works like this:

```
element {
    background: background-color background-image background-repeat background-position
    background-attachment;
}
```

As an example, consider the following two rules that produce exactly the same output—a row of repeated animal crackers displayed on an orange background, along the bottom of a *div* with *id="hihopickles"* :

```
#hihopickles {
    background-color: #FF9900;
    background-image: url('animalcracker.png');
    background-repeat: repeat-x;
    background-position: left bottom;
    background-attachment: fixed;
}
#hihopickles {
    background: #FF9900 url('animalcracker.png') repeat-x left bottom fixed;
}
```

When applied to our document, our *hihopickles* element might look like the display shown below.

3-27. Hi Ho Pickles!

## Building Texture: Vintage, Patterned, Worn, and Nostalgic Styles

In review, the texture-related elements we've described so far are point, line, shape, depth and volume, and pattern. Individually, each of these components creates some level of texture. But when you begin to use them together, they build on one another to create more complex visual imagery. How you combine them depends on the type of effect you're trying to create. So, the question is: what is the textural effect you want to achieve? Let's look at a few options.

### Paper Grain

In 2019, Google released a side project called "The A-Z of AI"[14], which was designed to explain the basic concepts of Artificial Intelligence. The styling is modern and friendly, using broad panels of color, simple children's book illustrations, and big, expressive typography. But look closely at the flat color areas and you'll notice a papery graininess. I zoomed up a small area in the image below, but you may need to examine the real thing to fully appreciate this texture. It's subtle enough that most users probably won't consciously notice it, but it backs up the uncomplicated children's book style perfectly.

---

[14] https://www.misterretro.com/filters/permanent-press

3-28. The designers of Google's A-Z of AI project gave an essentially flat design a warm, tactile twist

How do they get this effect? I have to admit, I spent some time combing through the `background-image` CSS of all the large flat panel areas looking for a tiling graphic—but found nothing. It was only the next day that I had a little revelation. What if, rather than adding grain to each and every panel, they created a barely visible "grainy lens layer" that overlayed the entire site? Think of it like a Snapchat filter for graininess. Bingo! I'd been looking in the wrong place.

3-29. This is the noise graphic they use to get the grain texture (noise.jpg)

If you inspect the HTML, you'll find an `:after` pseudo element with the attached CSS:

```
._3rV4LQ0BePEq9V1dxEjhEF::after {
    background: url(/static/noise.jpg);
    content: "";
    height: 100%;
    left: 0;
    opacity: .05;
    pointer-events:""one;
    position: absolute;
    top: 0;
    width: 100%;
    z-index: 201;
}
```

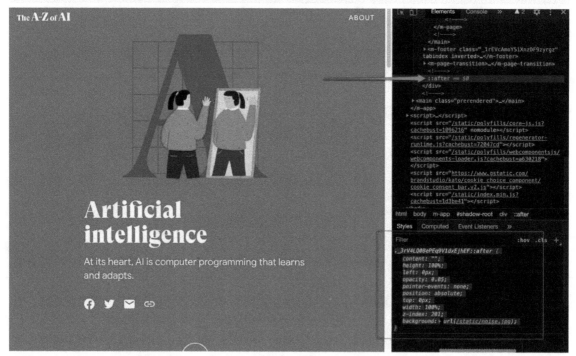

3-30. An :after pseudo element is attached to one of the main app containers

This layer uses the grain image ( `noise.jpg` ) as a tiling background, and they've positioned it to cover the entire screen ( `width:100%` , `height: 100%` , `top:0` , `left:0` , and `z-index:201` ).

As we suspected, the opacity is set to almost transparent ( `opacity: .05` ), so that all that remains is a hint of uneven grain. The only potential gotcha with covering the screen with a "lens layer" (even if it's transparent) is that it will block access to all the links, inputs, and other user interactions below it. However, this is easily solved by adding `pointer-events: none`, which makes this lens layer invisible to the cursor.

I think this is a really useful technique. It delivers site-wide visual impact using no more than one tiny graphic and a dozen lines of CSS. That's great bang for buck.

## Paints, Pencils and Other Traditional Media

Computers are built to be precise and clean, and unlike most traditional media, digital colors don't accidentally run or smudge or bleed or smear. This is great for keeping your desk clean, but it also means real, loose, organic, natural media like paint and pencils really stand out when you can find the right setting for them.

3-31. The More of Less campaign for Airbnb China brings Chinese watercolor into the digital world

New Zealand agency Resn[15] gives us a perfect example, authentically reproducing a traditional Chinese watercolor style to promote Airbnb experiences in rural China. This

15. https://www.resn.co.nz/

watercolor style permeates every pixel of the application, from dollying animation sequences to full-screen backgrounds, making it a huge undertaking.

## Faded Memories

When **Obys Agency**[16] paid digital tribute to Formula One ace Niki Lauda, their design approach leaned heavily on the mountains of fantastic archive photos and footage from Niki's career. The gravelly red-sepia photos give the site a warm, slightly wistful feel. It can be tempting to follow the retro theme too far, and perhaps mimic an old book or newspaper. Happily, Obys avoided this cliche by being able to showcase archive imagery within the kind of a dynamic web layout that's simply not possible in a traditional book.

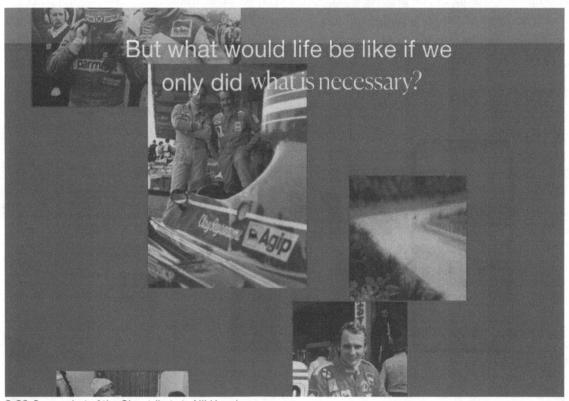

3-32. Screenshot of the Obys tribute to Niki Lauda

---

16. http://obys.agency/

## The Digital Retro Look

3-33. Hypebeast adds a big spoonful of 1982 to their mix of music and streetwear

Of course, "retro" isn't a time, but a perspective, as <u>Hypebeast</u>[17] demonstrates with their 1980s take on the retro theme, above. Their spinning vortex, two-color linework and glowy scanlines evoke visions of *Tron* light cycles, *WarGames* strategic command centers, and *Blade Runner*.

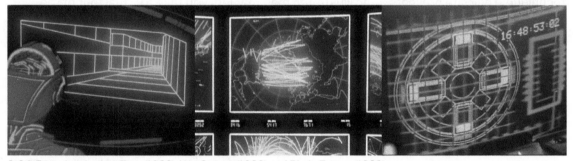

3-34. Retro inspiration: Tron (1982), WarGames (1983) and Blade Runner(1982)

Although Hypebeast have used HTML5 canvas to render their animations, this "glowy TV scanline effect" would be perfectly suited to the lens layer technique we dissected earlier in the chapter.

## Halftone and Ben Day Dots

If you've ever looked closely at any comic book, newspaper or magazine, you've probably

---

17. https://hypebeast.com/2019/8/ozweego

noticed the pattern of dots creating the tone in images. Technically, there are two types of dot patterns in print. **Halftone screens**[18] create an image by varying the size of each dot. The first panel of the figure below shows a halftone sample from a <u>1964 Andy Warhol mural</u>[19].

**Ben Day**[20] **dots** are slightly different. Comic books—like the Superman example shown below —typically take black linework art and drop in areas of flat, evenly sized Ben Day dots to simulate extra ink colors. A grid of small red dots on a white base is a cheap way to get pink. Although the grungy, stippled look of these techniques began as an accidental byproduct of the print process, eventually it became an artistic statement in its own right—and continues to be used that way today.

3-35. Halftone and Ben Day dots in Warhol's pop art, newspaper ads and comic books

The small Japanese village of <u>Misato, Shimane</u>[21], gives us my favorite recent example of this technique. Their site presents as an illustrated map that lets you take a virtual tour of the village. The illustrations are fun and mostly flat color but with some wonderful halftones, adding depth and texture.

---

18. https://en.wikipedia.org/wiki/Halftone
19. https://en.wikipedia.org/wiki/Thirteen_Most_Wanted_Men
20. https://en.wikipedia.org/wiki/Ben-Day_dots
21. https://www.town.shimane-misato.lg.jp/misatoto/

3-36. Misato, Shimane, uses chunky halftones to give flat color illustrations depth and bite

## DIY Halftones

There are dozens of Photoshop filters that will mimic the halftone process on your images (including <u>Mister Retro</u>[22], who we mentioned above). They're fine, but if we're going to flush image detail out of a photo by converting it to a halftone, in my view it makes sense to convert it into a vector graphic—ideally an SVG we can use online. For this, I can happily recommend <u>HalftonePro</u>[23].

---

[22.] https://www.misterretro.com/filters/permanent-press/halftone-effects
[23.] https://halftonepro.com/app

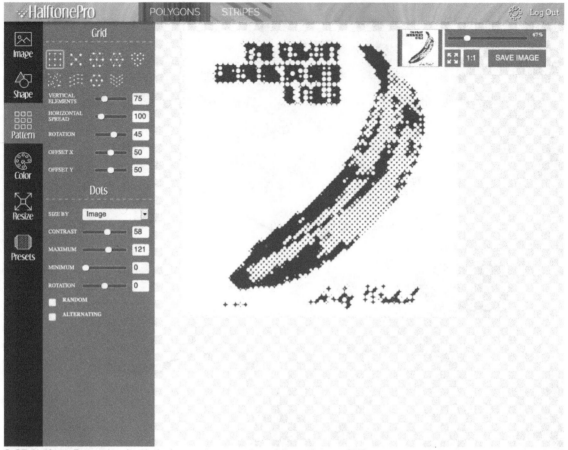

3-37. HalftonePro makes it relatively easy to convert any bitmap into an SVG

HalftonePro lets you upload any bitmap and apply a raft of halftone settings, including:

- grid scale
- grid pattern (circle, square, triangle, etc.)
- dot shape (circle, square, triangle, etc.)
- contrast
- color output

Here are some tips for making good halftones:

1. Not all images are suited to this style. Bold, high contrast images are generally more successful.

2. File sizes can get big and unruly if you select a very fine grid. Embrace the grunginess.

3. Use the presets to begin with to help you get a feel for what works.

3-38. Four different halftone treatments applied to The Velvet Underground's Andy Warhol

HalftonePro isn't free. It's currently a $15 outlay, but note that this is a *one-time* payment for *lifetime membership*—in a world full of monthly or yearly subscription plans. I paid for it and still think it's good value.

### Starting Your Own Textural Trends

As illustrated by the websites we've featured above, texture can have a big impact on how people perceive your design. Staying on top of current web design trends is essential for creating effective contemporary designs, but having a knowledge of past modes that occurred outside the ethereal history of the Internet will help you to establish your own style and original designs.

Some of the most useful web design resources can be found in the art history section of your local bookstore or library. Becoming familiar with the architectural patterns of the High Renaissance, investigating the Realist movement (and understanding how it influenced artists like Van Gogh and Cézanne to break all the rules on texture in paintings), and learning how modernism set the course for the design trends of today will help you do more than answer Jeopardy questions. A knowledge of graphic design history will expand your visual toolbox, giving you the creativity to develop a style that's all your own, and the artistic variety to suit any client's needs.

Ultimately, the image that your clients are trying to establish, and the communication goals they've set, should be the determining factors in how much and what types of texture you apply.

## Application: Adding a Design Motif Using SVG Patterns

In Chapter 2 we resolved to limit our color palette so our design wouldn't clash with or detract from the art being displayed. What other methods are there to add some visual distinction to our design? The great museums and art galleries of the world have the same challenge, so perhaps we can pinch some ideas from them?

One trick I've noticed is they often develop some kind of simple design **motif** not dependent on color—a shape, design, pattern or texture they can reuse and repurpose without having to worry about a preset color palette. Two killer examples are shown below.

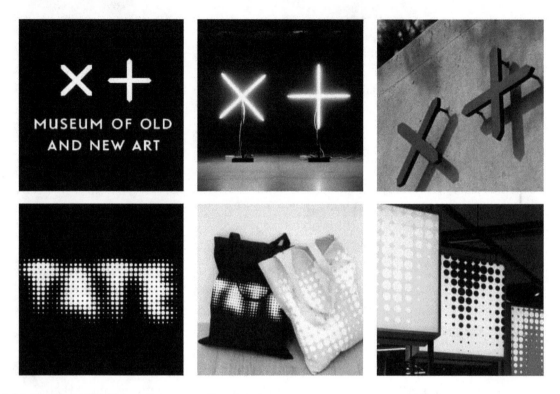

3-39. Top row: MONA, Hobart. Bottom row: Tate Galleries, London

The top row shows the branding used by the amazing Museum of Old and New Art (MONA[24]) in Hobart, Tasmania. That "X+" shape isn't just a logo. It's used continually throughout the building, the grounds and even on the ferry terminal that takes you there. It's even punched into metal as a repeating pattern. It works in almost any size, color or building material.

The bottom row shows how London's Tate[25] galleries repurpose their grungy halftone brand in everything from cloth bags to ticket booths. Sure, the base logotype is the word "TATE", but it's often cropped so hard that it switches from being legible text to a purely graphic motif.

While we may not have the budget, time or—let's face it—mad skills of the MONA and Tate design teams, we might try to develop a motif of sorts for our project using the color palette we settled on in the last chapter.

---

24. https://mona.net.au/
25. https://www.tate.org.uk

# Using a Pattern as a Motif

Vector applications like Figma, Sketch, Adobe XD, and Illustrator are great tools for leveraging the geometry of patterns. Symbols (known as "components" in Figma) make manipulating pattern elements much easier because edits to the "parent" pattern shape are passed on to the child shapes instantly.

I'm going to start with a set of concentric circles as a base unit, and then I'm going to overlap three of those units like fish scales. If I make a vector mask to isolate half of the visible part of the back-most circle (that is, the blue area shown below), we now have a versatile little tile that we can convert into a reusable symbol (or component) in your graphics editor.

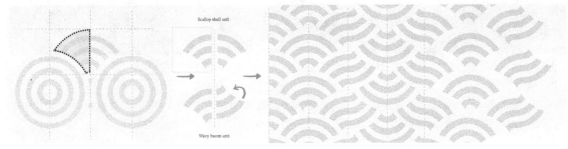

3-40. Creating a tile unit for use in patterns

If we mirror a duplicate of that tile along its vertical axis we get that original "scallop shell" unit. However, if we simply rotate a duplicate of the tile 180 degrees and fit those flat edges together, we get what I'm calling the "wavy bacon" unit. Wavy bacon fits perfectly into the scallop shell. The right edge of that wavy bacon matches perfectly with an upside-down scallop shell. And so on …

We now have an interesting pattern that we can use:

- with any color palette
- in high contrast or subtle faded versions
- in border trims or full background panels

And because everything is based on our original tile symbol, any changes to color, scale, tone, or contrast in that symbol ripple through the entire pattern immediately.

Although the easiest option is to simply export a PNG to use as a seamless background tile, SVG has some fantastic, built-in `<pattern>` properties that let you build super-efficient vector patterns, which is what you see below (below).

3-41. An SVG pattern like this is sharp at any scale, and tips the scales at a feather-weight 1.5KB

Diving deeply in SVG pattern code is perhaps best left to another book, but if you're interested in the code, feel free to tinker with the **CodePen demo**[26] I used when building it.

For now, it's time for us to move on to the next chapter of this design adventure: typography!

# Typography

Chapter

**4**

Let's face it: the core purpose of all web design is communication. Whether we're talking about an online retail store, a web presence for a Fortune 500 company, or a profile for a social networking site, typography is a vital component of your message. For most people, typography is simply about arranging a familiar set of shapes to make words, sentences, and paragraphs. But ironically, having the ability to set type with only a few mouse clicks or strokes on a keyboard has allowed us to forget about the creative and artistic possibilities of this medium.

There are numerous obstacles to the effective customization of typography for the Web—and I'll address these in the coming pages—but the power of type should be motivation enough to push the proverbial envelope. Unconvinced? Pick up a magazine, turn on a television, or take a walk through a grocery store. You'll undoubtedly see hundreds of creative and effective uses of type. It's the substance of branding, the key to unspoken communication, and an essential piece of the web design pie.

 **This Topic May Be Addictive!**

After studying typography for some time, you'll never look at a billboard, brochure, or book the same way again. You might start snapping pictures of ride signage at theme parks rather than of your kids. Pondering whether the entrées in a restaurant menu are set in Cantoria or Meyer Two may become more interesting than choosing between the entrées themselves. The study of typography is one that draws many people in … and never lets them go! Consider yourself warned.

In order to unlock the potential of type, we must first understand it. Admittedly, this is no easy task. The minute details of letterforms and the spaces around them have been carefully calculated over centuries of investigation and practice. In the early days of print, every letter of every typeface had to be carved into wood or cast from lead, inked, and then pressed into paper. This was a professional craft requiring exacting attention to detail. Even though the physical craft has long been surpassed by modern printing methods, many colleges and universities offer classes in letterpress, so that future graphic designers can both appreciate the benefits of working with type on a computer and see the potential for typographic exploration.

My personal love of typography is twofold. As a designer, I enjoy working with type for the artistic aspects of it. I like the unique voices that different fonts provide, and the expressiveness of type like the example below After all, the root words that comprise typography are *typos* , meaning impression or mark, and *grapheia*, meaning writing. **Typography** literally means making impressions with writing. As a programmer, I also appreciate the puzzle-like problem solving that working with type involves. The choices of font and color are only the tip of the type iceberg. In fact, the majority of the decisions that need to be made in our work with type involve the space *around* the letterforms and text blocks, rather than the actual type itself. Nevertheless, choosing an appropriate typeface is a crucial step.

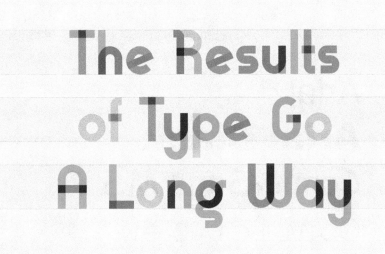

4-1. The Gilbert color typeface (typewithpride.com) proudly shows off its own construction

The history and implementation of type is a topic that's filled hundreds of books. In this chapter, though, I'll merely provide a brief introduction to the world of typography. First, I'll cover some of the issues with—and solutions for—taking type to the Web. Then we'll examine some basic typeface terminology, explore some usage guidelines, and investigate the characteristics of different fonts. From our discussion of legibility concerns, to the question of using dynamic headings online, I hope you'll find this chapter to be practical and inspirational.

If you like what you see here, and would like to explore the rabbit hole a little deeper, here are a few web resources I highly recommend:

- *The Elements of Typographic Style Applied to the Web*[1]
- *Practical Typography*[2]
- *Typewolf*[3]
- *I Love Typography*[4]
- *Typographica*[5]

---

[1] http://webtypography.net/
[2] https://practicaltypography.com/what-is-typography.html
[3] https://www.typewolf.com/
[4] http://ilovetypography.com/

## Taking Type to the Web

When it comes to the Web and choosing fonts for text that will be displayed in a browser, it doesn't matter if you have five or 5,000 fonts installed: you have to think in terms of the lowest common denominator.

The number of font families that are supported, by default, across both Mac or PC is very small. This list of nine font families below is commonly known as **web safe fonts**.

Arial

**Arial Black**

Comic Sans MS

Courier New

Georgia

**Impact**

**Times New Roman**

Trebuchet MS

Verdana

4-2. The nine "web safe" fonts that are installed by default on both Windows and macOS: Arial, Arial Black, Comic Sans MS, Courier New, Georgia, Impact, Timers New Roman, Trebuchet MS, and Verdana

The downside to the safe list is that there's limited variety within each font category. If you need a standard sans-serif font, you have to choose between Arial, Trebuchet MS, and Verdana. (If you're not sure what "sans-serif" means, jump ahead to the section called "Typeface Distinctions" for an in-depth look at the different categories of fonts.) For someone who hasn't been exposed to many fonts, that may seem like a reasonable variety, but for those of us who know the nuances of other sans-serif fonts like Helvetica Neue, Futura, and

---

5. http://typographica.org/

Univers, using one of the safe fonts can be like using a screwdriver to drive in a nail.

Fortunately, the `font-family` property of CSS allows you to choose multiple fonts in order of preference. This is referred to as a **font stack**. If the first font is unavailable, the second font will be used; if the second font is absent, the third font will be used; and so on. Let's say you want your section headlines to have a serif font. You think the best font for the job is Calisto MT, so you specify that first—for the few people who have it installed. Your second choice is your first backup plan, and for this you choose Georgia. If users don't have Calisto MT installed, they'll see Georgia. Even though Georgia is on the safe list, some people may not have it installed. Times New Roman is a close equivalent, so you decide you might as well add it as your next alternative. To finish off the preferential list, to cater to users who don't have any of those fonts installed, you add what the W3C calls a **generic font family**. The generic font families are `serif`, `sans-serif`, `cursive` (similar to script or hand lettering), `fantasy` (or novelty), and `monospace`. All your font choices so far have been from the serif family, so that's the generic family you specify. In summary, your font stack would look like this:

```
.class {
    font-family: 'Calisto MT', Georgia, 'Times New Roman', serif;
}
```

 **Font Names with Spaces**

> Any font family names that include spaces should be quoted, either using single ( ' ) or double ( " ) quotes (see the quotes around Callisto MT and Times New Roman in the code above). This is long-standing best practice, so even though it's not strictly necessary (see Mathias Bynens[6] on this topic), it's best to stick with it, just to be safe.

The key to creating an effective font stack is knowing which fonts are most similar and, more importantly, which ones are installed by default in each operating system. CSSFontStack.com[7] (below) helps you make decisions by providing useful data on the current state of the world's typographic ecosystem.

---

6. https://mathiasbynens.be/notes/unquoted-font-family
7. https://www.cssfontstack.com/

CSS Fonts
From **Dan's Tools**

▾ Web Dev ▾ Conversion ▾ Encode/Decoders ▾

A complete collection of web safe CSS font stacks.

# Sans-serif

| Arial | | Arial Black | | Arial Narrow | | Arial Rounded MT Bold | |
|---|---|---|---|---|---|---|---|
| ■ Win: 99.84% | ■ Mac: 98.74% | ■ Win: 98.08% | ■ Mac: 96.22% | ■ Win: 88.39% | ■ Mac: 94.77% | ■ Win: 59.53% | ■ Mac: 95.14% |

| Avant Garde | | Calibri | | Candara | | Century Gothic | |
|---|---|---|---|---|---|---|---|
| ■ Win: 0% | ■ Mac: 1.08% | ■ Win: 83.41% | ■ Mac: 38.74% | ■ Win: 83.08% | ■ Mac: 34.41% | ■ Win: 87.62% | ■ Mac: 53.15% |

| Franklin Gothic Medium | | Futura | | Geneva | | Gill Sans | |
|---|---|---|---|---|---|---|---|
| ■ Win: 99.18% | ■ Mac: 2.1% | ■ Win: 1.26% | ■ Mac: 94.41% | ■ Win: 2.08% | ■ Mac: 99.64% | ■ Win: 58.54% | ■ Mac: 95.5% |

| | | Helvetica | | Impact | | Lucida Grande | |
|---|---|---|---|---|---|---|---|
| | | ■ Win: 7.34% | ■ Mac: 100% | ■ Win: 0% | ■ Mac: 95.14% | ■ Win: 0% | ■ Mac: 100% |

| Optima | | Segoe UI | | Tahoma | | Trebuchet MS | |
|---|---|---|---|---|---|---|---|
| ■ Win: 2.52% | ■ Mac: 93.69% | ■ Win: 75.36% | ■ Mac: 0% | ■ Win: 99.95% | ■ Mac: 91.71% | ■ Win: 99.67% | ■ Mac: 97.12% |

| Verdana | |
|---|---|
| ■ Win: | ■ Mac: |

4-3. The CSS Font Stack from Dan's Tools provides a useful snapshot of the current typographic landscape

## Self-hosted Web Fonts

Because the Web requires fonts to be presented in a special format that's different from your computer's font formats (a discussion for a different book), you can't just upload a TTF file from your computer to your web server and link it in your stylesheet. What's more, doing so would most likely violate your End User Licensing Agreement (EULA) with the font's foundry. If you want to host your own fonts, they'll have to be licensed for web embedding. You'll also need several different font formats, and you'll need the latest code for embedding all those formats. That's where <u>Font Squirrel</u>[8] (shown below) comes to the rescue. On this very useful site, you'll find hundreds of excellent free fonts, downloadable kits for embedding those fonts into your sites, and a generator that can convert your own font files into all the required web formats.

If you're unable to find what you're looking for in Font Squirrel's collection of free fonts, visit their sister site, <u>Fontspring</u>[9]. Here you can purchase commercial fonts from actual font foundries who allow `@font-face` embedding, many of which offer an unlimited domains license for a small surcharge.

## Acherus Grotesque AaBbCcDdE
| 🖵 🌐 | Acherus Grotesque | Horizon Type | 2 Styles | | DOWNLOAD OTF (OFFSITE) |

## Eurocine AaBbCcDdEeFfGgHh
| 🖵 🌐 | Eurocine | Paulo Goode | 2 Styles | | DOWNLOAD OTF (OFFSITE) |

## INTRO RUST ABCDEFGHIJKLMN
| 🖵 🌐 | Intro Rust | Fontfabric | 3 Styles | | DOWNLOAD OTF (OFFSITE) |

## *Milkshake AaBbCcDdEeFfGgHhIiJj*
| 🖵 | Milkshake | Laura Worthington | 1 Style | | DOWNLOAD OTF (OFFSITE) |

4-4. A selection of the vast array of free fonts available at Font Squirrel

## Web Font Services

If you'd rather not bother with all the font files and ever-evolving code for embedding them, there are several services that host the fonts and keep up with the embedding nuances for you. With each of these services, you simply pick a font, grab a snippet of code to drop into your site, and voilà!—your type is displayed in that font.

Let's look at a few of the better-known ones.

---

[8.] http://www.fontsquirrel.com/
[9.] http://www.fontspring.com/

### Google Fonts[10]

As with many of their services, Google have slowly but surely become the default choice for hosted web fonts. They have an easy-to-use UI, a monster CDN backbone, and are currently closing in on 1,000 font families on offer. They also don't rely on the service to pay the bills, so unless they get bored, Google Fonts is probably your safest long-term option.

### Typekit[11]

Typekit was the original hosted font solution, developed by Jeffrey Veen and Jason Santa Maria and now owned and operated by Adobe. The service has built strong relationships with a number of leading type foundries, giving it a selection of high-quality, distinctive type products. Typekit offers a free trial library for a single site. Otherwise, their pricing is based on a yearly subscription that varies based on page views per month.

### Hoefler & Co.[12]

Hoefler & Co. is a New York type foundry founded and run by rock star type designer Jonathan Hoefler. They offer an exclusive selection of original typefaces via a yearly subscription service, either via their cloud service or a "host-your-own" option.

### Brick[13]

Brick offers a small but well-curated collection of quality free fonts ready to be linked from your site or web app. According to their site, they count Runkeeper, Buffer and Playlistas clients, so that gives me some confidence in their staying power.

### Font Library[14]

Font Library is always worth a look. You'll definitely find a lot of fonts you won't find elsewhere. The quality of the individual fonts varies more than some of the services listed above, but you may find just the font you need.

Now, you may be wondering if font-hosting services like Google Fonts have made CSS font

---

10. https://fonts.google.com/
11. https://fonts.adobe.com/typekit
12. https://www.typography.com/webfonts
13. https://brick.im/
14. https://fontlibrary.org/en

stacks redundant. Well, not at all. The reality is that externally hosted fonts fail. Technology has a habit of glitching. Sometimes the files get withdrawn or moved or blocked by a proxy or bandwidth restrictions. By all means choose attractive, interesting typography—but also think carefully about your fallbacks when things inevitably go wrong.

## Anatomy of a Letterform

Some of the design classes I took in college delved fairly deeply into the anatomy and terminology of type. Many people can already identify serifs, ascenders and descenders, but for one class, we had about 100 terms to memorize. While I'll be nicer here, it's important that you know some basic terminology before we continue learning about type. Sure, I *could* just talk about type using informal words like "squiggles", "slants", and "thingies" to describe letterforms, but that could grow confusing rather quickly.

The figure below represents an example of each component of a typeface. We'll go over them in turn below.

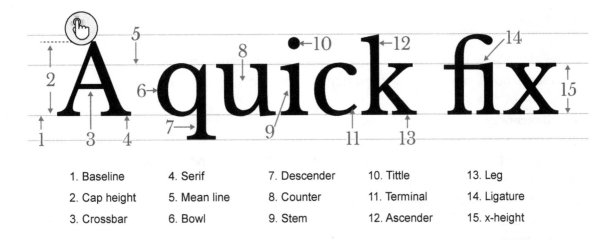

| | | | | |
|---|---|---|---|---|
| 1. Baseline | 4. Serif | 7. Descender | 10. Tittle | 13. Leg |
| 2. Cap height | 5. Mean line | 8. Counter | 11. Terminal | 14. Ligature |
| 3. Crossbar | 6. Bowl | 9. Stem | 12. Ascender | 15. x-height |

4-5. The terminology of type

### 1  Baseline

The **baseline** is the imaginary horizontal line on which most characters sit. The only character that hangs below the baseline above is the lowercase "q".

### 2  Cap height

The **cap height** or **capline** is another imaginary line. This one marks the height of all capital letters in a typeface. Notice that the cap height is below the maximum height of the typeface.

### 3   Crossbar

A stroke that connects two lines in the capital letterforms of "A" and "H" is called a **crossbar**. A horizontal stroke that doesn't connect two lines, like the one in the lower case "f" or "t", is known as a **cross stroke**.

### 4   Serif

**Serif** is the name given to the finishing strokes at the bottoms and tops of certain typefaces. I'll talk more about serifs when we cover typeface distinctions.

### 5   Mean line

Another imaginary horizontal line that marks the top edge of the lowercase letters is the **mean line** (or **midline**). Despite what its name might imply, the mean line isn't always exactly centered between the baseline and the cap height.

### 6   Bowl

The **bowl** of a letter is the rounded curve that encloses negative space in a letterform. Examples of bowls can be seen in the letters "D", "o", and "g".

### 7   Descender

The lower portion of a lowercase letter (such as "g", "j", "p", "q", and "y") that extends below the baseline of a typeface is known as the **descender**. The only other characters that typically extend below the baseline are the old-style numerals in some typefaces. These types of numerals—examples of which can be seen in the Georgia typeface below—were thought to blend better with lowercase roman numerals. They also look particularly good when used within a body of text.

# 1567 1567

4-6. Old-style numerals in the Georgia font on the left, and standard numerals in Helvetica on the right

### 8  Counter

The negative space within a letter is called the **counter**. In some letters, like "A", "o", and "P", the counter is fully enclosed. The non-closed negative spaces in letters like "G", "u", and "c" are also known as counters.

### 9  Stem

A stem is the main vertical or diagonal stroke in a letterform. These include the vertical portions of the letters "I" and "H", as well as all the strokes in the letter "W".

### 10  Tittle

This is probably my favorite typeface term. **Tittle** is the name given to the dot above the lowercase "j" and "i".

### 11  Terminal

The end of a stem or stroke that has no serif is known as a **terminal**. Even the ends of some serif typefaces have terminals, as you can see in the letter "c" above.

### 12  Ascender

Some lowercase letters have an **ascender**, which is an extension that rises above the mean line. Those letters are "b", "d", "f", "h", "k", "l", and "t".

### 13  Leg

The lower angled strokes seen in the letters "K", "R", and "Q" are known as **legs**. These are also sometimes referred to as **tails**.

### 14  Ligature

You may have noticed that the "f" and "i" of the word "fix" are combined into a single character. This joining of characters is known as a **ligature**. Most ligatures fall into one of two categories. The majority solve a recurring spacing problem between two characters. More recently, coding font designers have used ligatures to substitute common multi-character sequences (such as `-->` or `<=`) with their single-character mathematical symbols, as the image below illustrates.

| | Roboto (sans-serif) | Fira Code (monospaced) |
|---|---|---|
| No ligatures | **fisticuffs** | **code  --><= := /=** |
| Ligatures | **fisticuffs** | **code  ⟶ ≤ := /=** |

4-7. Examples of ligatures in the fonts Roboto and Fira Code

### ⑮ x-height

Simply put, **x-height** is the vertical space occupied by the lowercase "x" in a given typeface. More accurately, it's the distance between the baseline and mean line that defines the body of lowercase letterforms—excluding ascenders and descenders. X-height is a key factor in typeface identification, and typefaces with larger x-heights are generally regarded as being more readable. Although it's impractical, you can actually use x-height ( *ex* ) as a relative unit of measurement in CSS.

## Text Spacing

Now that you know how to describe the parts of a letterform, the next step is to be able to define and adjust the space between letters. I mentioned before that many typographic decisions are based on spacing. This has always been true with printed type, and became applicable to web type with the advent of CSS. Regardless of whether we're talking about using type for print or for the Web, there are two directions in which we can control spacing: horizontally and vertically.

### Horizontal Spacing

Kerning and tracking are two terms you'll often hear in conversations about horizontal letter spacing. **Kerning** is the process of adjusting the space between individual letters. Often when you're working with type, you'll notice pairs of letters that appear too close together, or too far apart.

Most fonts have a set of rules that determine the spacing between specific characters. The kerning between the letters "Wa", for instance, should be—and is—much tighter than the kerning between the letters "WV". Most of the time, the rules for the font are sufficient to make the text readable. Otherwise, you can adjust the individual letter pairs within your image creation software of choice. The image below shows examples of text with no kerning applied, automatic kerning, and manually adjusted kerning.

No Kerning

Automatic Kerning

Manually Adjusted

4-8. AWE-inspiring kerning examples

For the text in a web page, it's impossible to make letter-by-letter kerning adjustments. What you *can* do is adjust the `letter-spacing` CSS property, which is known in the print world as adjusting the font's "tracking". Like kerning, **tracking** adjusts the horizontal spacing between letterforms, but applies to the space between each letter. If you want your text to have a more open, airy feel, try adding a bit of letter spacing as I've done below.

**Default Letter Spacing**  *(Tracking)*

Lorem ipsum dolor sit amet, consectetur adipiscing elit. Convallis ac metus gravida felis. Nunc enim gravida id habitant. Velit enim tortor massa consequat, a at. Pharetra amet gravida maecenas viverra pellentesque tortor donec in in. Ultrices at blandit porttitor suspendisse cras pellentesque nunc facilisis. Feugiat condimentum ut pellentesque ac auctor. Et sagittis vivamus faucibus et, risus tempor id ullamcorper ipsum. Lacus enim.

**.01em Letter Spacing**  *(Tracking)*

Lorem ipsum dolor sit amet, consectetur adipiscing elit. Convallis ac metus gravida felis. Nunc enim gravida id habitant. Velit enim tortor massa consequat, a at. Pharetra amet gravida maecenas viverra pellentesque tortor donec in in. Ultrices at blandit porttitor suspendisse cras pellentesque nunc facilisis. Feugiat condimentum ut pellentesque ac auctor. Et sagittis vivamus faucibus et, risus tempor id ullamcorper ipsum. Lacus enim.

4-9. A letter-spacing example

Another horizontal spacing option in CSS is provided by the `word-spacing` property. This property can take a positive or negative length, or the keyword `normal`. As you might expect, it affects the amount of whitespace between words.

## Vertical Spacing

In print design language, the vertical space between lines of text is known as **leading** (pronounced "**led**-ing"). This term comes from the early days of letterpress, when blank strips of lead were used to separate lines of metal type. When there were no added spacers, the lines were said to be set "solid". Text with added vertical space is much easier to read. As you can see in the first paragraph below, the default spacing between lines of text is too small. Ideally, you want the line height on your body copy to be about one-and-a-half times the size of your text. So if you have `12px` text, `18px` is a good, readable line height.

In the second paragraph, we've adjusted the CSS `line-height` property to `1.5em`. An **em** is a CSS unit that measures the size of a font from the top of its cap height to the bottom of its lowest descender. Originally, the em was equal to the width of the capital letter M, which is where its name came from.

**Default Line Height (1.1em)** *(Leading)*

Lorem ipsum dolor sit amet, consectetur adipiscing elit. Convallis ac metus gravida felis. Nunc enim gravida id habitant. Velit enim tortor massa consequat, a at. Pharetra amet gravida maecenas viverra pellentesque tortor donec in in. Ultrices at blandit porttitor suspendisse cras pellentesque nunc facilisis. Feugiat condimentum ut pellentesque ac auctor. Et sagittis vivamus faucibus et, risus tempor id ullamcorper ipsum. Lacus enim.

**1.5em Line Height** *(Leading)*

Lorem ipsum dolor sit amet, consectetur adipiscing elit. Convallis ac metus gravida felis. Nunc enim gravida id habitant. Velit enim tortor massa consequat, a at. Pharetra amet gravida maecenas viverra pellentesque tortor donec in in. Ultrices at blandit porttitor suspendisse cras pellentesque nunc facilisis. Feugiat condimentum ut pellentesque ac auctor. Et sagittis vivamus faucibus et, risus tempor id ullamcorper ipsum. Lacus enim.

4-10. An example of "leading" (or "line height" in CSS)

# Text Alignment

Have you ever noticed that the text you see in books and magazines is often aligned along both the left- and right-hand sides of the page or column? This type of text alignment is known as **justification**. When text is justified, the letter and word spacing is automatically adjusted so that each full line of text has a word or letter that lines up against the left and right edges of the text area. Many print designers will use justified text for any text block that's over two lines long and is wide enough. You can take this same text treatment to the Web with CSS by setting the `text-alignment` property to `justify`. Before you go and justify the whole Internet, though, let me give you two warnings about justified text.

1   A river runs through it.

Occasionally, a gap created by wider spacing in one justified row will line up with a gap in the next row, and the next, and the next … and you end up with a canyon or **river** in your type, as shown below. This can be distracting for the reader. Print designers can makes adjustments to fix this sort of problem, but on the Web, it's difficult to predict and impossible to fix.

2   What. Are. You. Saying?

The river problem is even more pronounced with narrow columns. Words will often be isolated against the left and right margin, or stretched over the entire width of the column. Most word-processing programs fix this problem by hyphenating words where necessary. Browsers are unable to do this kind of auto-hyphenation, so web designers should avoid using justified text in narrow spaces.

> Lorem ipsum dolor sit amet, consectetur adipiscing elit. Arcu pretium orci, nunc vitae urna. Vulputate ridiculus at scelerisque egestas at sit quis mi placerat. Pretium sodales viverra eget odio sociis commodo ipsum commodo. Arcu, a iaculis volutpat tellus. Odio feugiat purus id in nulla cursus lectus tristique.
>
> Justified text and narrow columns, particularly narrow columns with longer words do not play well together either

4-11. Justification problems: when you stretch text to the edges, fractures begin to develop in the middle

If you don't want to change the `text-alignment` of your text to `justify`, your other options are `left`, `right`, or `center`. When text is centered or aligned along the left or right edge of the page or column, the spacing between the characters and words remains constant. The river problem can occur with any text block, but it's much less likely to cause legibility issues in text that's centered or justified on one side only.

## Typeface Distinctions

Everybody knows what a **font** is. It's a set of letters (or characters) that appear in a certain style. Fonts come pre-installed on your computer. And you change the font when you want your text to look different. The average Windows PC has just over 40 fonts installed by default, while the average Mac user has access to around 100 fonts. Many of these fonts are grouped together into font families, with each font within the family representing a different variation of the core font. Most font families include the regular font face, along with italic, bold, and bold italic variants. Some fonts have no variations at all, some may only have bold or italic, and some commercially available font families have hundreds of variants.

 **Font? Typeface? What's the difference?**

A family of fonts is called a **typeface**. For example, Times New Roman is a typeface. It's a collection of fonts, including Times New Roman Regular, Times New Roman Italic, Times New Roman Bold, and so on. Some typefaces include a vast array of fonts. If you're choosing a typeface for the Web (or for print), make sure it includes the font variations you require. Some beautiful typefaces don't include any variations for bold or italic text, for example, meaning you'll get disappointing results if you need bold or italic text.

Just as all the members of some families have big ears or abnormally long pinkie toes, every font family has its own unique, identifiable characteristics. Take a look at the variation that exists between fonts for the letter "g" below.

4-12. Look Ma! I'm pulling fourteen Gs!

These characteristics are what help us to categorize fonts and font families. The majority of font families can be classified as either serif or sans-serif. Of the 14 different fonts represented in the image below, seven could be classified as serif and seven as sans-serif. Can you distinguish between them? Beyond this distinction, there are many other ways in which we can classify and group fonts. I prefer to group fonts into six simple categories: serif, sans-serif, handwritten, monospace, novelty, and dingbats. Let's look at each of them now.

## Serif Fonts

Historians believe that the serif has its origin in Roman stone carving. There is much debate over the original purpose of these ornamental strokes, but in more recent history, they've been proven to increase legibility in large blocks of text by providing a horizontal line of reference. When many of us think of a serif font, Times New Roman is often the first one that comes to mind. However, there's a great variety of serif fonts on offer. To help us choose one, it's a good idea to first decide what type of *voice* we want our text to have.

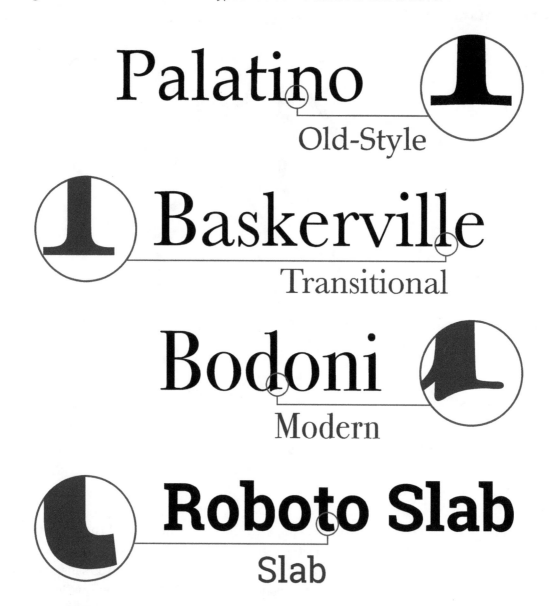

4-13. Four categories of serif

Take a look at the Palatino text above. Palatino is an **old-style serif** font. Old-style serif fonts are adapted from the brushstrokes of Italian scribes, and can be recognized both by the smooth transitions between thick and thin strokes, and by their rounded serif edges. Old-style serif fonts exude historic, handcrafted charm. At the same time, fonts like Garamond are extremely versatile: they're not so old-fashioned that they're unusable in modern applications.

The second font pictured above is Baskerville, a **transitional serif** font. The curved angle that connects the terminal of the stroke to the serif is known as a **bracket**. The brackets of transitional serif fonts are rounded, but the edges of the serifs are squared off. The simple addition of 90-degree angles and perfectly straight lines gives this category of font a more modern and mechanical voice. This category of serif fonts is known as **transitional**, because it provides a transition between old-style and modern serif fonts.

The third font, Bodoni, is known as a **modern serif** font. Modern serif fonts use a more pronounced contrast between the thick and thin strokes, and their serifs are often completely unbracketed. Modern serif fonts were introduced during the Industrial Revolution as a radical alternative to the transitional serif style.

Ironically, today these fonts have a much stronger association with a timeless elegance and sophistication than the cutting-edge modernity of their birth. Because of the delicacy of their lightest linework, modern serif fonts are generally only suitable for use in headlines. The consistent use of Italian Didot and Playfair Display[15] in *Vogue* magazine[16], shown below, helped to establish both the font and the magazine as icons of style. Other famous magazines that use modern serif font faces for their mastheads include *Brides, W, Elle, Parents, Seventeen*, and *Harper's Bazaar*. They're fairly uncommon in web design, but are certainly a classy choice if high style is what you're aiming for.

---

[15] https://www.fontsquirrel.com/fonts/playfair-display
[16] http://www.vogue.com/

**VOGUE** Didot

EDITION AUSTRALIA ∨

FASHION   BEAUTY   BRIDAL   CULTURE   CELEBRITY   VOGUE LIVING   MISS VOGUE    SUBSCRIBE

Lato

#StayHome

FASHION FIGHTS BACK    PROTECT YOUR MENTAL HEALTH    SOCIALISE FROM HOME    WORKOUTS FOR SMA

Cover star   Playfair Display

VOGUE AUSTRALIA

CAREY MULLIGAN
interviewed by
MARGOT ROBBIE

FASHION
TO UPLIFT

INTERVIEWS

*Margot Robbie interviews*   Playfair Display
*Carey Mulligan on the*

4-14. Modern serifs lending a classy feel to Vogue

In the later part of the 1800s, as advertising, posters, and flyers became more common, a bolder variation of modern serif fonts was needed to catch people's attention. It was at this time that **slab serif** fonts were first introduced. You can see an example of Roboto Slab above. Slab serif faces like Rockwell[17] and Bodoni Egyptian[18] have an industrial but friendly voice that's far less snooty than modern serifs, and even more contemporary. Because most slab serifs were designed to be readable from a distance, they make for excellent headlines and

---

[17.] https://docs.microsoft.com/en-us/typography/font-list/rockwell
[18.] https://www.fontspring.com/fonts/shinntype/bodoni-egyptian-pro

have had bouts of popularity on the Web. The image below shows an example of slab serifs in action. Harewood Estate's[19] choice of Bodoni Egyptian Pro gives a nod to the tradition of a grand English estate house without appearing stern or unwelcoming—an unconventional but clever choice.

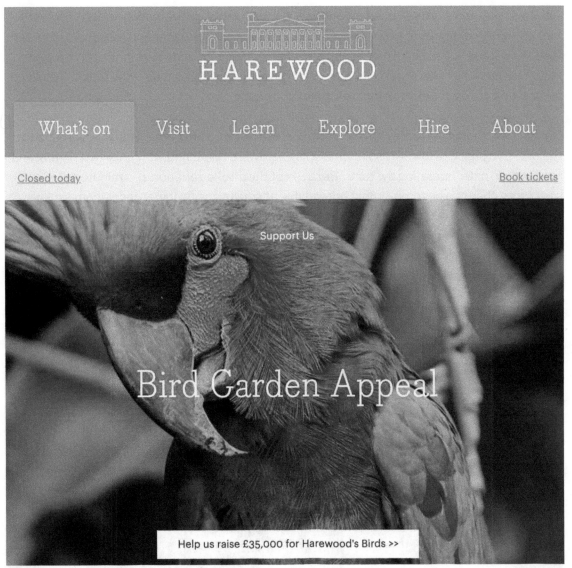

4-15. Slab serifs at Harewood House

## Sans-serif Fonts

**Sans-serif** fonts are fonts with no serifs at all. When typographers began experimenting with slab serifs, the idea of eliminating the serif altogether seemed like a huge mistake. Serifs were

19. https://harewood.org/

a tradition, so removing them was typographic castration. The initial sans-serif fonts were so loathed in the 1800s that they were referred to as grotesque. Eventually, though, people began to warm to the idea of serif-less typefaces, and by the 1920s some speculated that the serif would soon be eliminated.

Although serif fonts are still used extensively, the popularity and versatility of the sans-serif font category continues to grow. These types of fonts have a cleaner and more contemporary feel. They stand out as headlines, especially when paired with body text that's set in a serif face. This has long been a standard practice in print design, and is a tip I was taught in college for creating contrast between headlines and body copy.

On the Web, though, the roles have been reversed for a very long time. This is mainly due to the one-two punch of lower-resolution display hardware combined with poor text hinting and rendering in older operating systems. Because of the stroke variation and minute detail of serif fonts, they can become almost unreadable at small sizes on lower-resolution displays. As the pixel density of displays has increased and older computers die off, we've been freer to choose whether to serif or not to serif. The image below shows how <u>Kubrick.life</u>[20] pays tribute to the great film director's eye for dramatic shape and contrast by using <u>Acumin Pro's</u>[21] broad sans-serif letterforms as a mask.

4-16. Kubrick.life uses Acumin Pro's large, flat surface areas as an image mask

---

[20] https://kubrick.life/
[21] https://fonts.adobe.com/fonts/acumin

Regardless of how they're used, sans-serif fonts are extremely legible and practical for almost any purpose. The most ubiquitous sans-serif fonts on the Web are Arial and Verdana. Each of these font families exists in the default font sets of both major operating systems, and, as a result, they're predictably the workhorses of web body copy. In the design world, these families have a reputation for being overused and generic (and in the design community, Arial has the added stigma of being widely considered the poor cousin of Helvetica). Sometimes a stronger serif font, or a more distinguished sans-serif font, will do the trick, but there are certainly many more options available outside these two categories.

## Handwritten Fonts

Before the invention of movable type systems, all text had to be carved, brushed, or written by hand. The downside to handwritten text—especially my own—is that achieving a uniformity of letterforms, alignment, and spacing can be frustrating. And, as a result of these challenges, handwritten text can be very difficult to read. Yet the wonderful aspect about handwriting is that it acts as a symbol of humanity, giving a tangible personality to the text it represents.

Sacramento - Designed by Astigmatic

*The quick brown fox jumps over the lazy dog*

Permanent Marker - Designed by Font Diner

**THE QUICK BROWN FOX JUMPS OVER THE LAZY DOG**

Great Vibes - Designed by TypeSETit

*The quick brown fox jumps over the lazy dog*

Homemade Apple - Designed by Font Diner

*The quick brown fox jumps over the lazy dog*

Mr Dafoe - Designed by Sudtipos

*The quick brown fox jumps over the lazy dog*

Engagement - Designed by Astigmatic

*The quick brown fox jumps over the lazy dog*

4-17. Handwritten fonts ... for a human touch

Handwritten fonts provide a personal touch without the human error factor. The lettering and alignment in a handwritten font will be consistent, and if the font is well designed, the spacing should be good, too. As you look around at handwritten fonts on the Web, you'll probably start to think that anyone and their cousin's dog could create one, and it's true.

Unlike serif and sans-serif faces that require practice and precision, handwritten fonts are all about personality. If you want to create a font from your own handwriting, there are plenty of tools and services out there. One of the simplest sites for this is Calligraphr[22]. You simply print out a template, inscribe your glyphs on the grid, photograph it, upload it, and then download an OpenType format font file.

---

22. https://www.calligraphr.com/en

Calligraphr even supports <u>OpenType Contextual Alternates</u>[23], a feature that allows you to design and mix in multiple variations of any letterform. This is particularly useful for common double-letter combinations like "ee", "oo", "nn", "ss", "ll", and "tt". When supported and <u>enabled</u>[24] in Sketch, Figma, InDesign, Photoshop, Illustrator, Affinity Photo, and even MS Word, this feature will guarantee repeating letters are never identical.

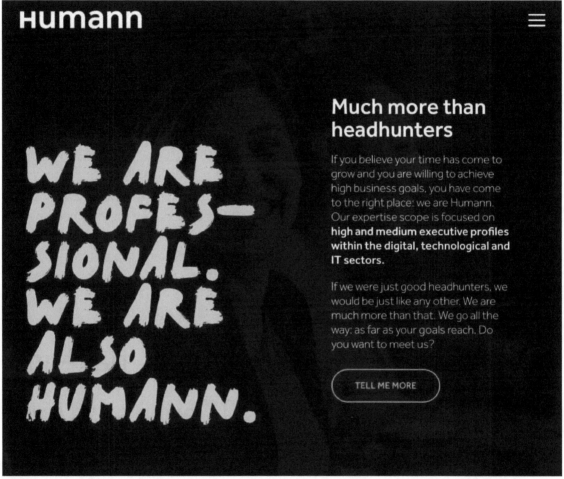

4-18. The "n" in Humann

In the image above, we see that Spanish recruitment agency <u>Humann</u>[25] have created their own impressive, hand-scrawled "Humann" font to give their company voice an unpolished but relatable tone. As effective as it is, contextual alternatives might have been especially useful here with such a raw, irregular typeface—and the continual occurrence of a double "n" in their company name (Huma**nn**).

---

[23]. https://www.typenetwork.com/news/article/opentype-at-work-contextual-alternates
[24]. https://medialoot.com/blog/how-to-enable-opentype-features-in-word-photoshop-and-illustrator/
[25]. https://humann.es/en/

## Fixed-width Fonts

You may have noticed by now that, in most fonts, each letter takes up a different amount of space. For instance, the capital "W" takes up a large area, while the letter "l" has a very narrow footprint. To illustrate this point in plain text, take a guess which of the sentences in the image below has more characters.

# Women of the world wear makeup
# The lily in the valley is tiny

Font: Lora

4-19. A proportionately spaced font, Lora, from Google Fonts

That was a trick question; they actually have the same number of characters! So why does the first sentence appear so much longer than the second? The explanation for this phenomenon is that the majority of fonts are proportionately spaced. Associated with each character of each font are rules that determine not only the width of the character, but also the amount of space that will appear around each character. Take a look at those two sentences again, this time displayed in the Courier font.

# Women of the world wear makeup
# The lily in the valley is tiny

Font: Ubuntu mono

4-20. A fixed-width or monospaced font, Ubunto Mono, from Google Fonts

The reason the two sentences appear to be the same width now is that Courier is a **fixed-width** or **monospaced** font. This category of fonts has uniform spacing, and the letterforms are designed so that they're similar in width. Fixed-width fonts were initially designed around the technical limitations of typewriters. Since early typewriters were incapable of moving the typed page a different distance when a "w" was typed, rather than an "i," specialized fonts were developed for these devices. These fonts had to remain readable, despite the spacing being the same for every letter. Early computer displays employed fixed-width fonts as well, but it was only a short time before computers were able to display much more legible, variable-width (or proportional) fonts.

So why are fixed-width fonts still around today? Mainly for the sanity of coders and accountants. When you need to write code or display data as text, it's helpful when characters line up from row to row and column to column. Because you're reading this book, you're probably already familiar with fixed-width fonts from writing HTML and CSS. Code-focussed sites such as <u>GitHub</u>[26] and <u>Codepen.io</u>[27] make great use of these monospaced faces in their code panels.

However, monospaced fonts aren't only a utilitarian choice. The monospaced <u>GT Pressura Mono</u>[28] lettering on <u>LegoVentures.com</u>[29] (below) stacks together like little bricks—an elegant design nod to the product that inspires the site.

4-21. Monospaced lettering is a tribute to the product inspiring the site, Lego.

26. https://github.com/
27. https://codepen.io/
28. https://www.grillitype.com/typeface/gt-pressura
29. https://legoventures.com/about/

**Fixed-width Fonts and the HTML** pre **Element**

In web browsers, text within `<pre>` … `</pre>` tags is displayed in fixed-width fonts by default (although you can change this via CSS if you wish). A handy way to display text in a fixed-width font is to wrap it with `pre` tags. `pre` is short for preformatted text, and the `pre` element preserves tabs, spaces, and line breaks.

The `pre` element is really useful for displaying code or tabular data on a website, because it preserves line breaks, tabs and spaces that are common in that kind of data. You can simply copy your original code or tabular data and paste it into your web page inside `pre` tags.

However, there's one gotcha. If your code includes tags like `<div>`, `<p>` and so on, you can't just paste them in with the rest of your code, because the browser will still render them as an actual element, rather than just displaying them as code. You'll need to replace any `<` characters with `&lt;`, the character code equivalent, and `>` characters with `&gt;`.

As with every other HTML element, `pre` elements can be styled with CSS. Apart from choosing the font to display in the `pre` element, web developers often give the `pre` a border, a background color or texture, additional margins, and various text treatments to help it stand out.

## Novelty Fonts

**Novelty fonts**, which are also known as **display**, **decorative**, or **fantasy** fonts, represent the vast majority of free fonts available online. Some of the fonts in this category are modified versions of popular serif or sans-serif fonts, and some are completely off-the-wall ideas that would be better described as conceptual art than a font face. By their very nature, these fonts are less legible than their traditional counterparts, but when used sparingly, they can add a wealth of personality and flair to a design. A few examples of novelty fonts are shown below.

4-22. Examples of novelty fonts available on Google Fonts

Often, novelty fonts are good starting points for a logo design or your site's main pitch text. Cyber-Duck's "How GDPR stole Christmas"[30] manages to channel some serious Dr. Suess vibes by using this wonderfully Grinchy typeface.

---

[30.] https://howgdprstolechristmas.com/

4-23. Cyber-Duck's "How the GDPR stole Christmas" infosite invokes Dr. Suess with their type

While I do know a thing or two about typefaces, I'm hardly a font-recognizing machine. Usually, if I come across an interesting string of text in an unfamiliar font, the first thing I think is WTF! I am, of course, referring to MyFont's excellent <u>WhatTheFont</u>[31] automatic font identification system. All you have to do is crop and clean up a text sample, upload it to WTF, and it will search for character matches in its database. The image below shows some of the matches for the "How GDPR stole Christmas" text above. WTF really is an invaluable tool, and if it fails to recognize your text, the site has a forum of "nerdy font detectives" who love to solve typographic puzzles.

---

[31.] http://new.myfonts.com/WhatTheFont/

4-24. MyFonts' WhatTheFont service

As with all design choices, before you use a novelty font, you should think about your client's requirements and target audience. Most clients will already have some form of branding in place, and choosing a bizarre or offbeat novelty font may tarnish the company's image. Even so, it's best to keep an open mind when you're coming up with themes for a website design. It may be that the company you're working with wants to stray from its corporate image.

## Dingbat Fonts

When you're looking for illustrations and artwork to incorporate into the design of a website, you should consider "dingbat" or "symbol" fonts. In the early days of print, **dingbats** were ornamental characters used to separate printed text and fill whitespace. Original dingbat fonts consisted mainly of flourishes and commonly used symbols. However, the concept of dingbat fonts changed radically with the digital font revolution. Now, any series of graphics can be assigned as characters in a dingbat font.

While these fonts may not be of much use from a typesetting perspective, they can be useful as supportive vector graphics and icons. Since fonts consist of scalable vector shapes, dingbat glyphs can be converted to outlines in Photoshop or Illustrator, and then resized, dismantled, and manipulated without any loss of quality. The only issue when using these fonts is that you have to know where to find the glyph you're after. Occasionally, I'll remember an arrow or symbol from a dingbat font, and type out half the alphabet before I find the one I want. Fortunately, though, most dingbat fonts have a theme, so it's easy to remember which font the glyph is in, even if the specific character is hard to find.

When people think about dingbats, the first sets that come to mind are Wingdings and Webdings, the dingbat fonts that come pre-installed in Windows. There are actually hundreds of other dingbat fonts available on the Web. A few examples are given below.

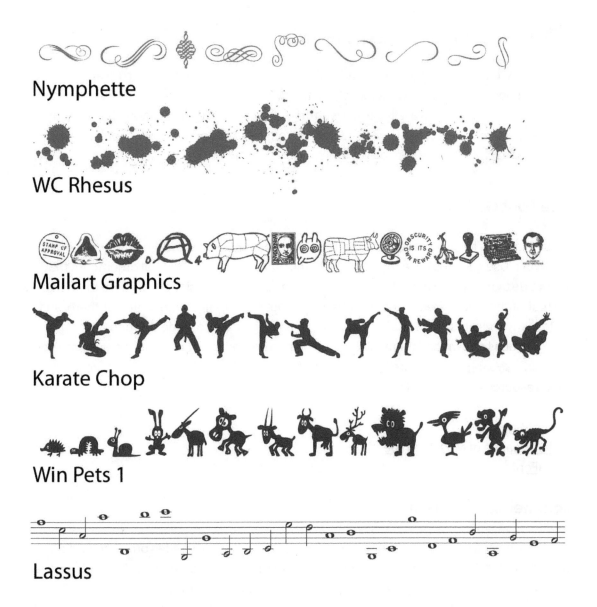

Nymphette

WC Rhesus

Mailart Graphics

Karate Chop

Win Pets 1

Lassus

4-25. A few examples of free dingbat fonts

## Finding Fonts

Although I've mentioned that you can find fonts on the Web a few times now, I've yet to really give you any places to look for them. If you start googling for fonts, you'll probably discover that there are three main categories of font sites out there: free font galleries, commercial font galleries, and sites for individual artists and foundries. All are great sources of fonts to add to your typographic tool belt.

**Desktop Fonts vs Fonts for the Web**

Before we proceed, just a reminder. As noted earlier, font files need to be available in specific formats to work reliably on the Web. If you're buying a font for use on the Web, make sure it's available in a web-friendly format. Often you'll see the webfont version of a typeface offered separately from the desktop version, so make sure you're choosing the version you really want!

## Free Font Galleries

These websites list and categorize free fonts from many designers. Some of the designers listed on these galleries have their own websites, through which they sell other fonts that they've designed. If you enjoy the fonts created by particular designers, be sure to track down the rest of their work. Remember that there are lots of really ugly free fonts out there, and while many websites claim to offer free fonts, you often have to wade through loads of annoying ads to download them. Also, if you plan to embed a font (even a free one) into your site using `@font-face`, be sure that the font's license allows it. With that said, here are a few great resources for free fonts:

- Font Squirrel[32]
- The League of Movable Type[33]
- DaFont[34]

## Commercial Font Galleries

Like the free and shareware galleries mentioned above, these websites promote fonts from many different designers and foundries. But unlike those galleries, most of the fonts here cost money. In most cases, though, you really get what you pay for with typography. If you license a font from one of these sites, as well as gaining a complete set of characters, the purchased fonts often include bold, italic, oblique, and other variants.

- FontShop[35]
- Monotype[36]
- Veer[37]

---

[32] http://fontsquirrel.com/
[33] https://www.theleagueofmoveabletype.com/
[34] http://dafont.com/
[35] http://fontshop.com/
[36] http://fonts.com/
[37] http://veer.com/products/fonts/

- MyFonts[38]
- Adobe Fonts[39]

## Individual Artists and Foundries

Many of my favorite contemporary fonts come from a handful of individual artists and companies. Most of these websites have a few free fonts, as well as offering fonts for sale:

- **Schick-toikka**[40]. This foundry offers beautiful, supremely useful, versatile fonts. I have a particular love for Noe.
- **Jos Buivenga's Exljbris.com Font Foundry**[41]. Jos is the creator of such popular typefaces as Museo, Anivers, and Diavlo.
- **Letterhead Fonts**[42]. This little foundry has over 200 high-quality, unique fonts with an early 20th century theme.
- **Blue Vinyl Fonts, by Jess Latham**[43]. Like many font designers, Jess started designing fonts as a hobby. His freeware and commercial fonts have a unique style and an emphasis on script styles.
- **Fountain Type, by Peter Bruhn**[44]. Fountain features some of the best fonts from about 20-odd designers around the world. The site also provides attractive freeware fonts.
- **Typodermic Fonts, by Ray Larabie**[45]. Ray has been a rock star in the free fonts world for a long time. His work is known for having high-quality character sets across a vast range of typographic styles.
- **Misprinted Type, by Eduardo Recife**[46]. Eduardo offers a tasty range of fonts with a particular penchant for theatrical pen scripts, distressed blockfaces and three-ring circus ornamental faces. His work is unmistakably unique, if a little twisted.
- **Pizzadude, by Jakob Fischer**[47]. Jakob makes fun, loose, irreverent typefaces and has cranked out over 500 handmade fonts since 1998.

## Choosing the Right Fonts

Even if you understand all the technical aspects of letterforms and typeface categories, and

---

[38] http://myfonts.com/
[39] "http://adobe.com/type/
[40] https://www.schick-toikka.com
[41] http://www.exljbris.com/
[42] http://letterheadfonts.com/
[43] http://bvfonts.com/
[44] http://fountaintype.com/
[45] http://typodermicfonts.com/
[46] http://misprintedtype.com/
[47] http://pizzadude.dk/

have access to all the fonts in the world, you can still have difficulty choosing the right ones. That's because font selection is based just as heavily on artistic license and emotional association as it is on technical issues. So, where do you begin?

In order to start your quest for the perfect font, you should first define the feelings you're trying to evoke in your target audience. Are you trying to show that the company the website represents is hip and young, or would you rather portray an aura of steadfast wisdom? Do you want to create a site based on a certain theme, like a Hawaiian luau or a Mexican fiesta, or are you trying to convey a more formal identity? By asking yourself these kinds of questions, and thinking about fonts on an emotional level, you should be able to decide reasonably easily whether a given font is appropriate for your application.

If you're unable to answer those questions about a particular font, make up your own questions. Sometimes the answer isn't always the obvious choice. Take a look at USA Networks Mr. Robot mini-site[48] (below). The series title uses the most harmless-looking fonts imaginable—a tribute to early-80s Sega that I couldn't have imagined *any* plausible use for. Yet it becomes truly sinister set against the dim rooms and palely lit faces of Elliot Alderson's world. This was an edgy type choice, but I believe it paid off in spades. Tellingly, they didn't overplay their hand by reusing the typeface throughout the site. The color choices and smaller type choices support the dark 80s vibe without needing to mimic it precisely.

---

[48.] https://www.usanetwork.com/mr-robot

4-26. Mr. Robot gives a fun 80s video game font a dystopic twist

Think about it: you've seen billions of letters and millions of words in your lifetime. So, whether you know it or not, you already have some emotional connections to base your font choices on. Think back to the logos, the album covers, the textbooks, and the signage you've seen. How have those typographic elements affected your perception of the entities they represent?

Now, let's take that idea and work backwards, using a generic entity like Joe's Restaurant. The font you choose for this design will play a crucial role in the way potential diners perceive the attitude and identity of the restaurant. Take a look at at the image below and try to choose some fonts that make you think of a casual Italian bistro. Okay, now pick fonts that suggest a metropolitan restaurant serving five-star cuisine. How about a tacky dockside bar? There's no right answer for any of these scenarios, but there are definitely some fonts that will outright fail to work in each case. First, try to narrow the field down to a few good candidates, and then try to refine your choices again, until you find one that works well.

| Joe's Restaurant | Joe's Restaurant | *Joe's Restaurant* | Joe's Restaurant |
|---|---|---|---|
| Skia | Versailles | Legault | Colona MT |
| JOE'S RESTAURANT | JOE'S RESTAURANT | *Joe's Restaurant* | **Joe's Restaurant** |
| Lithos Pro | Charlemagne | Park Avenue | Disgusting Behavior |
| **JOE'S RESTAURANT** | Joe's Restaurant | *Joe's Restaurant* | Joe's Restaurant |
| Umbra | Amigo | Sloop | Bubbledot ICG |
| Joe's Restaurant | Joe's Restaurant | *Joe's Restaurant* | JOE'S RESTAURANT |
| Insignia | Adobe Jenson Pro | Pelican | Cottonwood |
| **Joe's Restaurant** | Joe's Restaurant | Joe's Restaurant | **joe's restaurant** |
| Bauhaus 93 | Modern No. 20 | Harrington | Slugfest |

4-27. 20 different fonts to make you want to eat at Joe's

Keep in mind that, like kids, there are no bad ones—just regrettable choices. While a particular font might fail to work for one purpose, it may strike just the right chord in another situation. The trick is to try to keep an open mind. If you can narrow the field to a few possibilities, try asking a friend or co-worker the question, "Which one makes you feel more ___?", inserting the feeling you're aiming to elicit.

Finally, when you're choosing fonts, it's important to limit your selection. As a rule of thumb, try to use at least two, but no more than four, different fonts in a website design. Before incorporating a new font, remember that you probably have some variants (bold, italic, condensed, black, regular, and so on) at your disposal to vary your type while maintaining consistency. Try to also avoid combining two different serif fonts or two different sans-serif fonts in the same project. Like the discordant colors phenomenon I talked about in Chapter 2, placing different fonts from the same family next to each other in a design can feel eerily uncomfortable.

## Establishing a Typographic System

Setting up the typography for any sizable project is always complicated. There are literally hundreds of tweakable variables, and it's very easy to spend endless hours adjusting sizing, line heights, margins and weights. The best way to save your sanity is to have a design system that can generate quick answers to most of the little questions—which lets you concentrate the "big picture" decisions.

Often our first *big* typography decision is to set the body font size for our default layout. (Let's put responsive design to the side for now.) For many years, 16 pixels was considered the default body size of the Web. However, with today's larger screens, text-heavy sites such as blogs and news services are generally choosing 18- to 21-pixel body font sizes. Social media and ecommerce apps that use busier, more modular UI units have tended towards 14- to

16-pixel body fonts. Obviously, these are broad trends, and not hard and fast rules, but you can see these general trends in the list below.

### Typical Body Font Sizes

- Medium.com: *21px*
- NYTimes.com: *18px*
- CNN.com: *18px*
- Airbnb.com: *18px*
- SitePoint.com: *18px*
- BBC.co.uk: *16px*
- Developer.mozilla.org: *16px*
- Twitter.com: *15px*
- Etsy.com: *14px*
- Wikipedia.com: *14px*
- Facebook.com: *14px*

4-28. Body font-size samples for The New York Times, Medium.com, SitePoint.com and Wikipedia.com

Remember that these big internet properties do a lot of user testing, so put some thought into where your application fits into this list. When you've settled on your base text sizes, eye-test them on real screens, tablets and phones until you're happy with them as a starting point.

## Scaling Your Type

So, now you've set your body font size. How do you decide on the sizing of your titles, section headings, subheaders, lists and blockquotes?

For me, the answer used to be, "Umm … tweak it till it looks … kinda right." I'd scale up a heading, bump the weight a little, jog it a pixel up, … push it back down, … and back up again. Frankly, it was exhausting, because there were so many finicky little decisions and very few totally wrong answers.

**Type scaling**—sometimes called **modular scaling**—lets you use *simple* math to give you *simple* typographic answers. It allows us to set a single scaling ratio to generate all our font sizes while keeping them in harmony. It's like a musical scale for type sizing.

## Type Scaling in Practice

Let's start with a body font size of `18px`. That makes our default paragraph size `1em` (or `18px`):

```
body{font-size: 18px;}
p    {font-size: 1em; /* (or 18px) */ }
```

I'm going to set a type scale of `1.25`. To calculate my `h5` font size, I simply multiply my paragraph font size by `1.25`. That that's `1em * 1.25`, or `1.25em`:

```
h5 = p * 1.25 = 1.25em
```

Our `h4` headings would be the `h5` size multiplied by `1.25` (`1.25em * 1.25`) or `1.563em`. Continuing the process gives us something like this:

```
/* Using a type scale of 1.25 */
h5 {font-size: 1.25em;}  /* 22.50px */
h4 {font-size: 1.563em;} /* 28.13px */
h3 {font-size: 1.953em;} /* 35.16px */
h2 {font-size: 2.441em;} /* 43.95px */
h1 {font-size: 3.052em;} /* 54.93px */
```

If I decided that my `h1` headings felt a little oversized at that scale, I could bump my type scale down to `1.2` to get this result:

```
h5 {font-size: 1.2em;}   /* 21.60px */
h4 {font-size: 1.44em;}  /* 25.92px */
h3 {font-size: 1.728em;} /* 31.10px */
h2 {font-size: 2.074em;} /* 37.32px */
h1 {font-size: 2.488em;} /* 44.79px */
```

Okay, so I need a pocket calculator to size my text? Happily, no. There are some great tools that let you tweak and test type scales in generated CSS in real time. My favorite is Jeremy Church's Type-scale.com[49] (below), a tool that lets you quickly test different type scales and generate working CSS. There's even a dummy layout on the right panel to eye-test your work and a CodePen export option. This is a great foundation for your typography CSS.

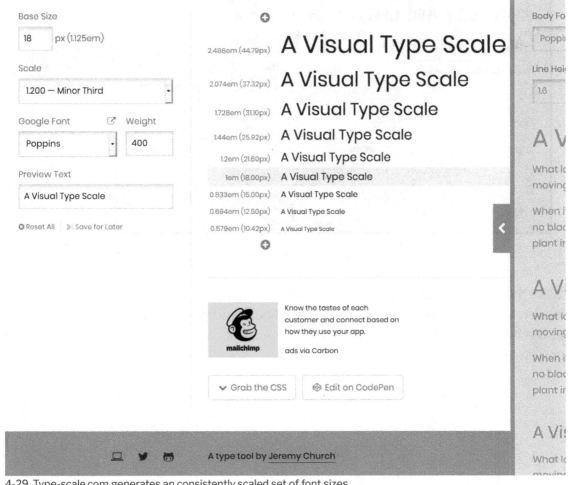

4-29. Type-scale.com generates an consistently scaled set of font sizes

## Mobile Considerations

A good question to ask at this point is, "Does a single type scale ratio work for all device sizes?" The answer is, no, often it doesn't.

If you compare the typography of a typical newspaper to that of a classic paperback novel (below), you'll notice some interesting differences beyond the obvious paper sizes.

---

49. https://type-scale.com/

4-30. Body type sizes are comparable, but headings scale much larger on larger formats

While their body font sizes may be quite similar, there's much great variation in heading sizes in the newspaper. Common sense tells you those headlines in *The Times* aren't going to work as chapter titles for *The Wizard of Oz*. As a general rule, smaller formats (such as phones and novels) need shallower type scales.

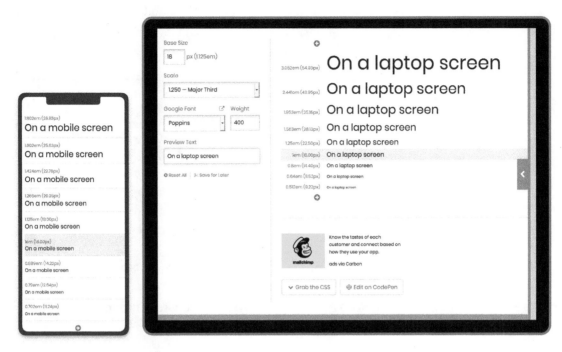

Type Scale: 1.125                                              Type Scale: 1.25

4-31. Larger format layouts can accommodate wider heading size variations

Note that this difference in type scales doesn't need to be large. As te image above shows, a small increase in type scale—from `1.125` up to `1.25` —ripples through the scale to generate a much larger top-level heading. While that `h1` title looks fine on a laptop, it would chew up far too much real estate on a mobile device. In short, it's wise to use CSS `@media` queries to serve two type scales—a steeper type scale for large screens, and a more compressed type scale for smaller screens. We'll tackle this later in the project.

So, now that we have a reliable, repeatable process to scale the type in our designs, let's look at the spaces *in between* that type.

## Vertical Baseline Rhythm

**Vertical baseline rhythm**—sometimes called the **vertical measure**—is a grid of horizontal lines that you can use to hang your typography in. It's not unlike the blue-lined school workbooks many of us learned to write in. The trick is getting your larger type units to fit into same grid as your body text. In a simple handwritten letter (below), E.G. Webb is allowing an extra row for his signature. He's probably using a baseline rhythm without even knowing what it's called.

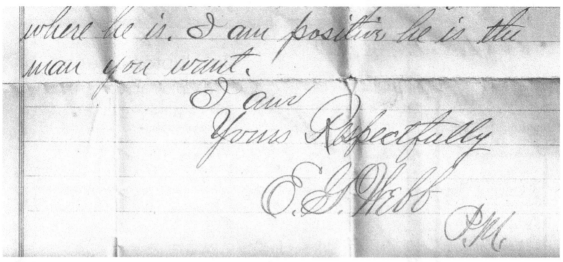

4-32. Regular horizontal lines help organize and regulate the text—even when the sizing changes

In *The Elements of Typographic Style Applied to the Web*[50], Richard Rutter describes baseline rhythm like this:

> *Headings, subheads, block quotations, footnotes, illustrations, captions and other intrusions into the text create syncopations and variations against the base rhythm of regularly leaded lines. These variations can and should add life to the page, but the main text should also return after each variation precisely on beat and in phase.*

How does that work on the web? Let's look at a real-world example. The excellent *Colossal magazine*[51] uses a very open, airy layout, yet it still somehow manages to feel strong and structural. How does it do that? It turns out that if we superimpose a $21px$ vertical grid over the whole layout (see below), we see a previously hidden structure emerge. For this example, I'm going to call one row of this grid a "unit".

You'll notice that:

- the site branding fits nicely into a box five units high
- the main navigation is three units high
- article titles are two units high
- secondary navigation and social links are one unit high

---

[50]. http://webtypography.net/2.2.2

[51]. https://www.thisiscolossal.com/

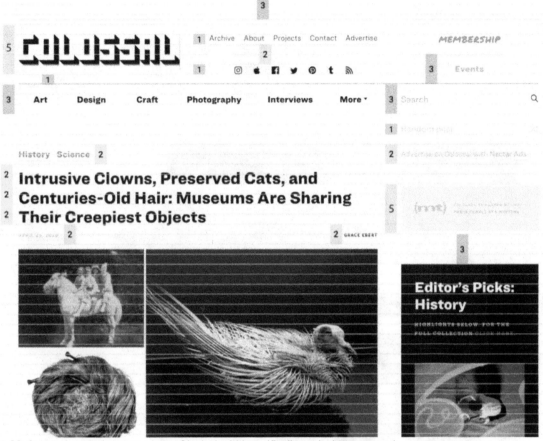

4-33. Colossal magazine uses a loose 21-pixel grid (specifically on desktop screens)

In fact, most UI elements "hang" on this underlying grid like socks pinned on an invisible clothesline. Even though we can't see the underlying grid, we're aware of it through a feeling of balance and harmony. It just feels right.

Note that we're not talking about just font size, but instead *the whole space the text occupies*—including the line height and margins. So in the *Colossal* example, the article title would have a line height of  *42px* , or two units for each line.

However, you'll notice that *not every* element is locked to this grid. The designers have chosen to offset elements like the photos from the grid. That's fine too. The grid is a great starting point, not martial law.

## Using Layout Grids

Most modern graphic layout tools (such as Sketch, Figma or Adobe XD) make it easy to add a vertical baseline to any canvas/frame. In this Figma example (see below), I selected the document frame and used the **+** button to add separate rows and columns in the Layout Grid panel.

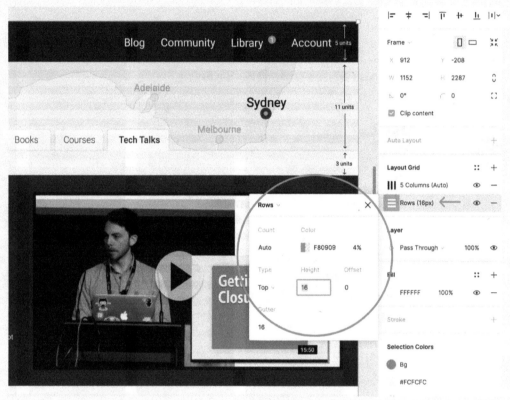

4-34. Layout grids in Figma help you make sizing decisions

These grid layers can be switched on and off using the eye icon. I find that, with a grid in place and "snap-to-grid" switched on, it simply becomes easier to size items with the grid than without it. And that makes your life easier.

There's even a tool to help you work out the CSS. Gridlover.net[52] (below) is an excellent, free tool that lets you experiment with different base font sizes, line heights and type scalings—all locked to a vertical baseline. If you try adjusting any of the line heights or margins on the right CSS panel, you'll notice the number only changes by a full "grid unit" each time.

---

[52] https://www.gridlover.net/try

4-35. Gridlover lets you try different base font sizes, line heights and type scales

You might also notice that the tool avoids using CSS padding in its typography. I've found this to be a good policy when working with a vertical baseline system. Use padding freely on your container units, but never on typography. Even text buttons can be given height with a line-height setting rather than CSS height or padding.

Gridlover not only writes useful CSS, but it really helped me get my head around how vertical baseline and type scaling can work in the real world. I believe this is a great place to start your CSS typography.

Archetype https://archetypeapp.com/ is another tool designed to help you create well-planned, integrated type systems. It offers controls for both type scale and baseline rhythm in one very thoughtfully conceived UI. It even encourages you to set different type scales for mobile and desktop out of the box. I believe this is the most sophisticated tool in this area.

The only caveat to Archetype is that it currently costs $59 per year to unlock the "Export as CSS" option. Clearly that's a bigger outlay than Gridlover (free), but if you spend a lot of time crafting type systems, it could save you a lot of time (and money). Archetype *is* very good.

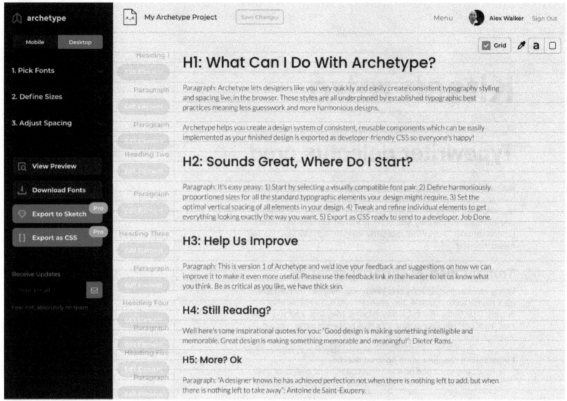

4-36. Archetype integrates type selection, type scale and baseline rhythm in a single UI

## Vertical Baseline Rhythm Is a Tool, Not a Religion

Vertical baselines are a handy tool, but they shouldn't become the end goal of your design. I have to admit, there was a time where I spent too much sweat trying to bend every page element to obey my mighty grid rules. I was arm-wrestling typographic percentages and margins, and "hitting the grid" became a goal in itself, rather than just a tool to help me design better.

That's neither fun nor useful.

Today, I think it's better to look at vertical baselines as a strong bass drum in a band—a regular beat that helps to measure out the space for the rest of the band to play in. Set up a nice backbeat that everyone can feel, but don't be afraid of dropping little off-beat flourishes. Often they can add energy and flavor to a composition (visual or musical).

Personally, I like to start with a strong grid and use it. If there's whitespace between headings or paragraphs, it might as well be one, two, or three whole "vertical units", rather than `1.3` or `2.75` units.

Likewise, your hero image might as well be *exactly* `12` units tall, rather than `11.8` or `12.3`, as now the bottom edge of the image is more likely to nicely line up with the bottom edge of any text flowing alongside it. It's "self-tidying".

But if, on the other hand, the caption on your images just looks too spacey when it's spread over 25-pixel line heights, that's fine. Forget the grid there. Just make it look good.

## The Takeaway

Ultimately, most design work is just a long, long list answers to "why" questions.

- Why did you make that major heading 49 pixels high?
- Why is that bottom margin 17 pixels?
- Why does the `h3` have a line height of `1.7778`?

And so on.

There are potentially hundreds of these little questions in even a small project. And you probably have enough natural "designer gut instinct" to answer them all—eventually. The problem is, it's *exhausting*.

However, if you can come up with a repeatable system that delivers viable answers to most of the boring, little questions, you can save your designer gut instinct for the bigger, more important questions.

Which is usually the fun part anyway.

## The Project: Building a Type System

Selecting typefaces for a project—like selecting a color palette—is always at least partly a personal choice. While there certainly *are* quantifiably bad choices, there's never just one correct answer.

This is a good opportunity to experiment with tools like <u>Fontjoy</u>[53] (below), which allow you to eye-test lots of different Google Fonts combinations and sizes quickly. Hit **Generate** to deliver a randomized combination. When you find a typeface you like, lock it in and regenerate the others.

---

53. https://fontjoy.com/

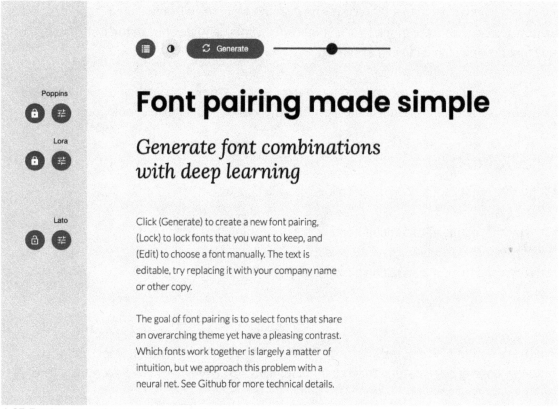

4-37. Fontjoy.com makes testing type combinations easy

For the Trashmonger project, I've settled on these fonts:

- **Poppins**[54] — a serious, Bauhaus sans-serif font
- **Lato**[55] — a warm, humanist body font

Google Fonts gives us this code snippet to add to our pages:

```
<link href="https://fonts.googleapis.com/css2?family=Lato:ital@0;1&family=Poppins:wght@300;500&
↪display=swap" rel="stylesheet">
```

We can load our new fonts straight into Gridlover.net (shown in green below) and begin to tweak the type scale and margins. I've set my HTML root element font size to  *14px* , and this is the only pixel measurement on the page. Every other font size, line height and margin will be set in rems. This means any change we make to that root element font size will automatically ripple through all the typography. This makes media queries much simpler.

---

54. https://fonts.google.com/specimen/Poppins
55. https://fonts.google.com/specimen/Lato

You'll notice that one row is always equal to `1.5rem` in this design, so that's the "magic number". Unless we have a good reason not to, all line heights and vertical margins should be multiples of `1.5rem`.

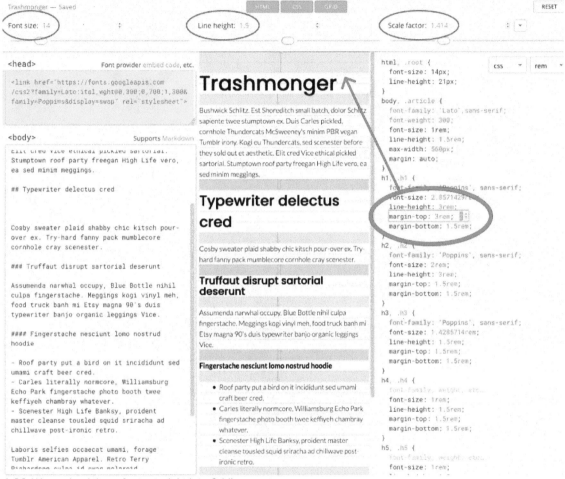

4-38. We can load these fonts straight into Gridlover.net

In the example above, I've used a type scale of `1.414` (Gridlover calls it the "Scale factor"), which is good for tablets and laptops. But, as we discussed earlier, we're going to export a second slab of CSS for mobile with a type scale of `1.25`.

## Creating a Basic Typography Style Guide

The next step is to put this CSS base into a simple one-page style guide. I find it's often easy to start this step in your favorite code playground (<u>CodePen.io</u>[56], <u>WebMaker.app</u>[57], and so

---

[56]. https://codepen.io/
[57]. https://webmaker.app/app

on) and move it inside your app/site later. Our base CSS will work something like this:

```css
/* Mobile first CSS (Type scale: 1.25) */

html, .root {
  font-size: 14px;
  line-height: 21px;
}
body, .article {
  font-family: 'Lato',sans-serif;
  font-weight: 300;
  font-size: 1rem;
}
'Lato'h1, .h1 {
  font-size: 1.9285714rem;
  line-height: 3rem;
  /* and so on ... */
}

@media screen and (min-width: 720px) {
  /* Tweaks for larger screens - Type scale: 1.4141 */
  h1, .h1 {
    font-size: 2.8571429rem;
    /* and so on ... */
  }
}
```

The mobile typography type scale is placed at the top of the file—as the default. A media query is set at 720 pixels to give us the steeper type scale font sizes, line heights and margins on non-phone screens. This relatively simple but robust core gives us a useful base for our typography. If we're not happy with anything, it's still easy at this stage to go back to Gridlover and tweak the type scale or line heights.

 **CodePen Demo**

Here's that core CSS set up as a simple CodePen demo: https://codepen.io/ SitePoint/pen/qBZbeKz. Scale the window to see the type scale switch between mobile and desktop modes.

## Adding a Visual Grid

You might also notice that I've added my own grid as an overlay. I find it really useful to be able to see the grid I'm working with as I'm building HTML prototypes. It's really easy to add and remove.

First, I set up two CSS variables at the top of my CSS file. We don't need the columns for this style guide, but they're ready when we do need them:

```css
:root{
  --columns: 5;
  --lineheight: 1.5rem;
}
```

Then I tack this CSS snippet onto the bottom of my CSS file. It uses CSS gradients that are sized to the line height to create a temporary grid overlay:

```css
.showgrid::after {
  display: block;
  position: absolute;
  content: "";
  width: 100%;
  height: 1000rem;
  opacity:.75;
  top: 0;
  left: 0;
  z-index:999;
  background: repeating-linear-gradient(
   /* columns */
     90deg,
     rgba(0, 0, 0, 0) 0%,
     rgba(0, 0, 0, 0) 5%,
     rgba(255, 0, 0, 0.05) 5%,
     rgba(255, 0, 0, 0.05) 95%,
     rgba(0, 0, 0, 0) 95%,
     rgba(0, 0, 0, 0) 100%
   ),
   repeating-linear-gradient(
     /* rows */ 0deg,
     rgba(0, 0, 0, 0) 0%,
     rgba(0, 0, 0, 0) 50%,
     rgba(0, 0, 255, 0.05) 50%,
     rgba(0, 0, 255, 0.05) 100%
   );
  background-repeat: repeat, repeat;
  background-position: 0 0, 0 0;
  background-size: calc(100% / var(--columns)) auto, 100% calc(var(--lineheight)*2);
}
```

You can add the grid to the *<body>* —or any HTML container—by simply adding the *.showgrid* class:

```
<body class='showgrid'>
...
</body>
```

Any time I want to turn the grid off, I just add a `-` temporarily to the class name (such as `class='-showgrid'`) and it disappears.

## What Now?

We now have a useful set of simple type units in a predictable structure. Later, if we decide we need more variation or different type scaling, we have a sensible system that we can easily extend.

So let's move on to Chapter 5, where we'll look at how imagery can combine with our new typography system.

# Imagery | Chapter
# 5

5-1. The Camera Eye

From layout, to color, to texture, to type, we've been talking about imagery since the beginning of this book. So why should there be a chapter dedicated to imagery alone, right at the end? As with typography, there are many practical concerns related to imagery that we need to cover—including file-type choices, image resolution, and photography sources. But naturally, there are also artistic aspects to this topic, and these deserve some detailed discussion.

The process of choosing photographic, iconic, and illustrative elements for a website design requires a basic understanding of the design principles we covered in the first few chapters. Take the image above for instance. I wanted to use an image of a camera at the top of the page as an iconic representation of the subject.

However, when I was looking for a suitable picture, my decision was based more on the angle of the image than the type of camera pictured. The direction the camera faces in this picture greatly affects the sense of movement on the page. If the camera were facing straight ahead, the page would look just fine, but it would *feel* static. If it were facing off to the right, your eye would gravitate off the page rather than into the content. This phenomenon is due to the rules of emphasis I talked about in Chapter 1. The placement of the camera at the top of this page helps to ensure it will be noticed. Isolating the image makes it stand out even more as a focal point. Finally, the direction of the lens creates a line of continuance that determines the next focal point of the page.

By the end of this chapter, you'll understand these concepts, and know how to apply them to your own designs.

# What to Look For

The old adage that a picture is worth a thousand words certainly holds true on the Web. Photographs and illustrations often serve as visual lures that catch passing visitors and reel them in to your content. On the other hand, the wrong images, or even a poor presentation of the right ones, can be detrimental to a website's appeal. Every viewer of a photograph or illustration sees that image differently, depending on the person's own background and individual experience. So the thousand words that one person draws from an image may be different from the thousand words another person takes from it.

Before you choose an image or illustration to include in the layout or content of a website, ask yourself the following three questions.

## Question 1: Is It Relevant?

Relevant images can add interest to your design and enhance the content of a web page. They provide visual bookmarks that help visitors remember what was covered on the page, and where to look when they return.

Take a look at the promo page for the **Bite eco-friendly dental products**[1]. Bite are asking customers to change a deep-seated habit: squeezing tube toothpaste and plastic brushes. So explaining the new habit in a single image is critically important. At first glance, their hero shot looks like a completely random jumble of items, but break the image down and you'll see they answer at least five important questions:

1. How big are the these tooth pills?
2. How many pills are there in a jar?
3. What does a bamboo toothbrush look like?
4. Does the handle detach?
5. What will the delivery look like?

This is, in fact, a very carefully composed photography that skillfully tells their story while also showing off a stylish product made from attractive materials.

---

[1.] https://bitetoothpastebits.com/

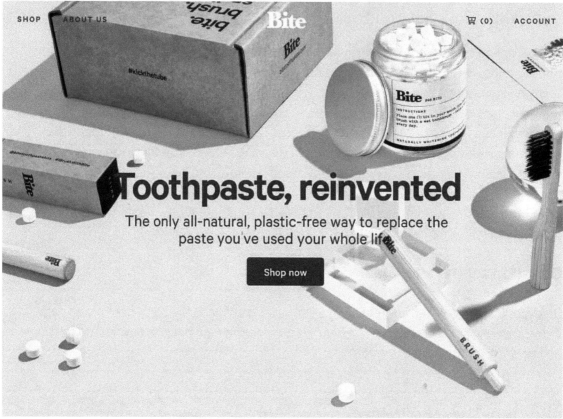

5-2. Bite: Toothpaste, Reinvented

## Question 2: Is It Interesting?

Your imagery doesn't even need to be beautiful to be effective, as <u>Julian Breheny</u>[2] shows us (no offense, Julian) with his personal site. Julian had to tackle the problem of showcasing his wide array of marketing, writing, video and design skills. The most obvious approach would be to create a portfolio spotlighting his best work. Unfortunately, this puts you in a "portfolio arms race" with every fantastic designer on the planet—which is a tough gig.

Instead, Julian designed and built a web app that asks clients to select only the skills they require, and then the app instantly rewrites Julian's "elevator pitch" to match their needs. This is no small feat. A typical site design requires one pitch and one hero shot. For this project, Julian had to create *62 pitches paired with 62 hero shots*. That's hours of spreadsheets, copywriting, preparation, studio time and execution.

However, if you're anything like me, you probably spent time clicking around looking for new combinations and visual gags. That's both engaging and memorable.

---

2. https://www.hi-im-julian.com/

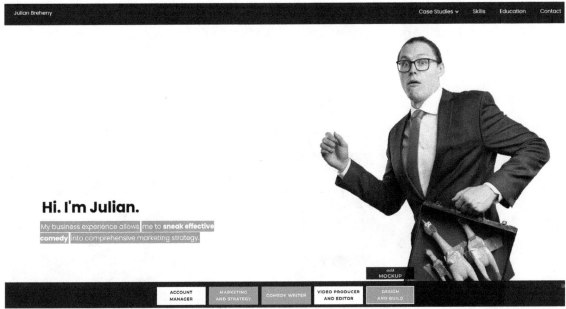

5-3. Julian Breheny shows us his sense of humor

The real beauty of Julian's approach is that the very act of creating the site perfectly showcases his:

- organization skills
- copywriting chops
- problem solving ability
- work ethic, and …
- comic timing

Frankly, it's hard to imagine any conventional portfolio site selling Julian's strengths more effectively that this site does. I salute you, sir.

## Question 3: Is It Appealing?

Images that are aesthetically or emotionally appealing can be a very efficient hook for attention and emphasis. The issue is that beauty and attractiveness are different for everyone. Depending on the subject matter and target audience of the site you're designing, an appealing image might be a portrait of a mother and her child, a panoramic cityscape, or an adorable cartoon mascot.

Appealing images are especially important for sites dealing with restaurants, recipes, and catering. If the food seen on the website fails to make your mouth water, customers will avoid eating, cooking, or ordering it. The photography on the St. Hubertus Restaurant site[3], seen below are rich, tactile and inviting. They create an atmosphere that makes you want to go there. There's one shot of somebody searing a marshmallow with a red-hot coal that has me convinced I can smell the burning sugar. Images like this don't just show the product, but also hint at a great experience awaiting you.

5-4. St. Hubertus showcases their experience with great photographic choices

I realize that relevancy, interest, and appeal are all very subjective, but sometimes subjectivity and artistic license are appropriate. If you think it's a good image for the project, run with it. Generally speaking, I'd avoid monsters, slime, and aliens in most websites, but as we've seen above, given the right client and target audience, it may be a valid design direction.

For every image you select for a design, you need to be able to answer "yes" to at least two of the questions above. Why not all three? Well, sometimes it's fun to toss in an appealing and interesting image that has nothing to do with your content—perhaps something as random as a bunch of birds carrying a whale in a net (the sadly departed Twitter "fail whale", shown below).

3. https://www.st-hubertus.it/de/#headerPage

5-5. Twitter's dearly departed "fail whale"

# Legitimate Image Sources

So, where does one acquire interesting, appealing, and relevant imagery to use for a website project? You basically have three options: create it yourself, purchase stock images, or hire a professional. The approach you take will depend on the budget and needs of your client, as well as your own skills.

## Take It or Make It

For me, taking pictures with my own camera or creating my own illustrations is usually a win-win situation. If local clients need pictures to use on their websites, it gives me a chance to escape the office and do something different for a change. I've had the opportunity to take pictures of products, restaurants, a factory, apartments, a martial arts studio, and storefronts. I was even able to ride around in a golf cart to take pictures of a golf course one morning, all while I was on the clock. But it's more than just a fun outing for me. Clients usually like the idea because it shows them that I want to be involved in every step of the project. It can also cost them less than it would to contract a professional photographer.

 **Photography Can Be Learned**

> While you may not think of yourself as a photographer, taking good photos is a skill that, like design, can be learned. A great place to start is SitePoint's _Photography for the Web_.

The same is usually true for illustration and animation work. Most of the time, a custom site design requires some level of illustration. For items like icons, buttons, backgrounds, basic drawings and logos, you might consider taking a stab at fulfilling the client's needs yourself. Keep in mind that illustration doesn't necessarily have to be complex or time-consuming for the message to be communicated successfully.

Take a look at the website for the agency __Designzillas__[4] below. The overlapping palm leaves create a lush, dappled jungle for their trademark cartoon dinosaur to erupt from. This simple dinosaur illustration has become a company mascot, following them through a number of site redesigns. The current site incarnation includes a pterodactyl, a hatching egg and three dinosaur appearances. Like Jeremy Breheny earlier, their imagery is used to emphasize fun and approachability over eye candy and awe.

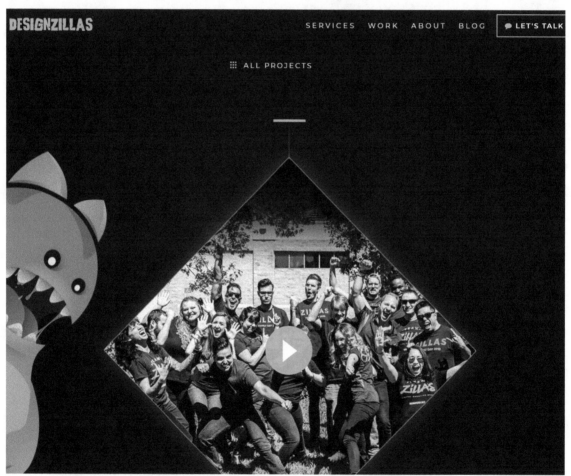

5-6. The ferocious Designzillas website, complete with attacking dinosaur

Occasionally, the do-it-yourself method doesn't work out for me. The illustration work the client needs might be outside my skill set, or it may be too complex for me to feel confident

4. http://www.designzillas.com/

taking it on. If it's a particular photo the client wants, I might lack access to the subject, or the quality of the image they need may be beyond the capabilities of my equipment. In those cases, my first instinct, and the next best option, is to turn to stock photography and illustrations.

## Stock Photography

If you're short on the time or ability to create or commission your own images, chances are that you'll find what you're looking for in a stock photo archive. These photo archives, or image banks, consist of photographs and illustrations that are created for general use, rather than a specific client or project. For a licensing fee (or sometimes for free), you can select any of these images for use in your project.

Finding the right images and photos for a design project can be a difficult task, depending on the subject matter and your budget. If your project requires pictures of animals, scenic vacation destinations, office supplies, or some random inanimate object, then you're likely to find what you're looking for easily. Every stock photo archive has these types of subjects well covered. Finding photos of people—like the girl with the unnaturally blue eyes and curiously long sleeves on the Brochure Ninjas[5] site—can be a little trickier. Most stock photo sites require that the photographer submit a signed model release for any image that includes a person's face.

---

[5.] http://www.brochureninjas.com/

5-7. Photos like this one at Brochure Ninjas can be more expensive

For this reason, you should expect to pay for good-quality pictures of people. Finally, if you need pictures of a product logo, current celebrity, or famous work of art, you have some work to do. Even though you may be able to find these sorts of images easily on search engines, using them for a professional project will likely require a very detailed licensing agreement.

 ## Always Look for Image Usage Guidelines

> Even if an image is restriction-free, you should ensure that your use of the image falls within the guidelines of the site's image licensing agreement. The guidelines for each stock photography source differ, so be sure you know what these are before you start looking for images. Some galleries even restrict their images to personal and nonprofit use.

The next question you must answer before you begin your quest for the perfect stock image is how much you're willing to pay. The price of using a single stock photograph can range from zero to hundreds of dollars. As you can probably imagine, the average quality of free images is dramatically lower than the quality of those you pay for. Free images can still be worth your while, though; you just might have to wade through a bunch of crummy pictures before you find what you're after. The same goes for expensive images. Just because you're willing to pay $500 for a single photo, there's no guarantee you'll receive a Ferrari instead of an early '90s Chrysler minivan with faux wood paneling. No matter what the licensing price of an image is, it all boils down to finding what you're looking for. If you can find it quickly, and at a great price, you'll have more time to spend on the design.

Three tiers of stock photography are available: free, royalty-free, and rights-managed. Let's look at each of these in turn.

## Free Images

I'm sure you've heard the saying, "There's no such thing as a free lunch". That principle could be applied to just about everything, and it definitely applies to the world of stock photography. Even though there are some excellent free stock images available, somebody is still paying for the equipment and the time it takes to create those images. Why would photographers do all this for free? For the same reason a talented musician might publish free MP3s, or a team of programmers might spend time on an open-source project. It's what they love to do, it allows many more people to enjoy their work, and it's an opportunity for their work to be noticed.

Of all the free stock photography sources out there, the one with the largest collection of free images, and the one that I use most often, is **Free Images**[6], pictured below.

---

6. http://www.freeimages.com/

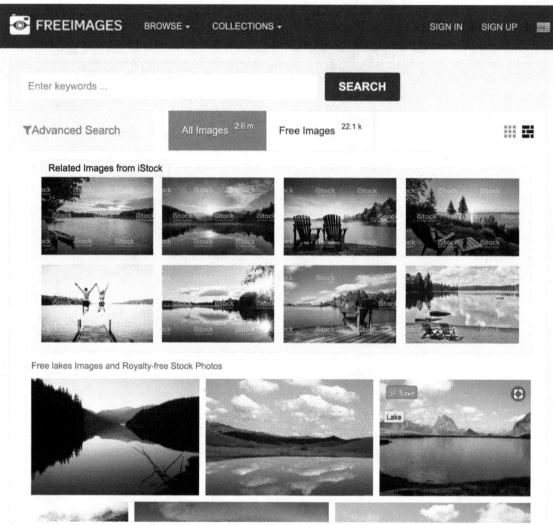

5-8. Free Images is a great source of imagery

Free Images has over 400,000 high-quality, user-submitted images. To ensure the quality and relevance of the gallery's database, site moderators check each submission before it becomes available. When you're downloading images from Free Images, be sure to check the restriction status of the image. Most images in the database are restriction-free, which means you can use them for most personal or commercial uses.

Other image resources worth checking out include:

- PxHere[7]
- New Old Stock[8]
- Pexels[9]

---

7. https://pxhere.com/
8. https://nos.twnsnd.co/

- ISO Republic[10]
- Unsplash[11]
- StockSnap.io[12]
- Picjumbo[13]
- SplitShire[14]
- NegativeSpace[15]
- Life of Pix[16]

The size of a stock photography collection plays a big role in how useful it can be. The more photos there are for a given search term, the more likely you are to find one that's useful. Although there are many free stock photo resources online, most of them have significantly fewer images, or the images they do have cover very specific, narrow topics. One such niche site for images is Old Book Illustrations[17]. The site has a large collection of scanned artwork and illustrations, like the image below, that are all old enough to be in the public domain. You can find a list of other sources for public domain images at Wikipedia's listing for public domain image resources[18].

---

9. https://www.pexels.com/
10. https://isorepublic.com/
11. https://unsplash.com/
12. https://stocksnap.io/
13. https://picjumbo.com/
14. https://www.splitshire.com/
15. https://negativespace.co/
16. https://www.lifeofpix.com/
17. http://www.oldbookillustrations.com/
18. http://en.wikipedia.org/wiki/Wikipedia:Public_domain_image_resources

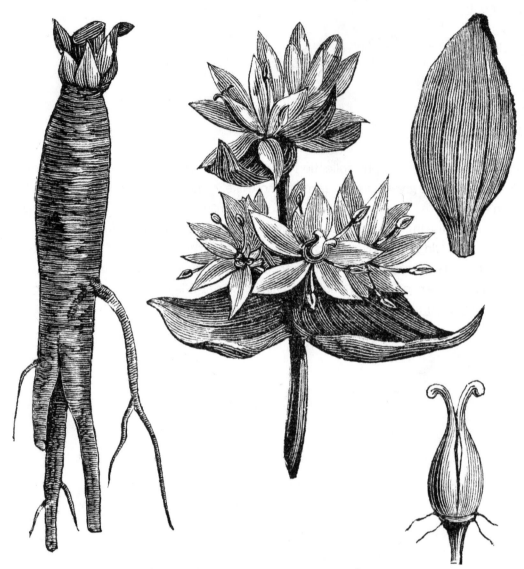

Gentiane jaune (*gentiana lutea*).

5-9. An image from Old Book Illustrations

In a similar vein, Flickr.com has mountains of royalty-free imagery if you know where to look. Over some two decades, hundreds of state libraries, museums, and government archives have digitized and uploaded their collections to Flickr as a public service. To be clear, most Flickr imagery is protected by copyright, but if you switch the licensing dropdown on the Flickr search page to "No known copyright restrictions", you'll unlock a treasure trove of old cartoons, engineering diagrams, maps, historical photographs, postcards and other assorted visual gems. You may have to dig, but there are some amazing images in there (and there's some super weird stuff, too).

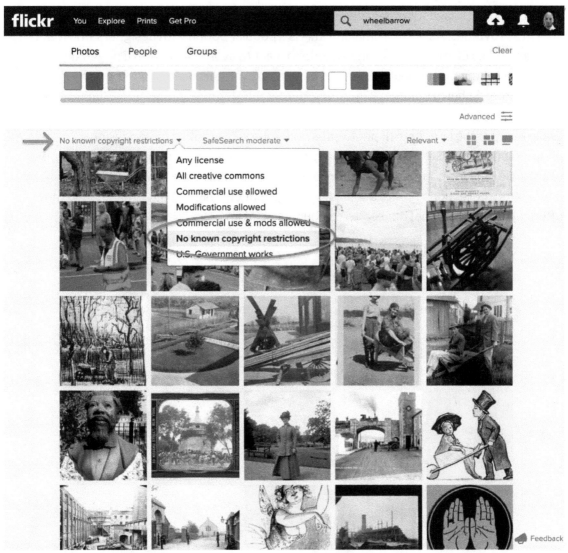

5-10. Flickr's "no known license" search

If you've spent any time looking for the right stock image, you'll know that finding what you need can be a frustrating experience. Sometimes you'll spend more time searching than designing, and when it's a client project you're working on, you simply can't afford to waste time. When you're willing to pay a little for the right image, the task of finding that image becomes much easier. That's when paid stock images come to the fore. They generally come in two flavors: royalty-free, and rights managed.

## Royalty-free Images

Contrary to what you might think, a **royalty-free** image is not available for use free of charge. The term refers to the details of the image's licensing agreement. A royalty-free image license is one that allows you to pay a single, up-front fee for an image. The payment buys you the right to use that image for other clients and projects without paying further licensing fees, known as **royalties**. As you can imagine, this is a popular option with designers who may need the same types of images again and again, and want to avoid the hassle of negotiating usage rights. One of the most popular places to purchase royalty-free stock photography is iStockphoto[19], shown below.

While many of the larger stock photo sites only source content from professional photographers, iStockphoto makes it easy for anyone to put their photos, illustrations, and even audio or video content up for sale. To maintain the quality and diversity of the iStockphoto collection, the site administrators accept only high-quality images, and they often reject offerings that duplicate the abundance of imagery they already have.

---

[19.] http://www.istockphoto.com/

5-11. An iStockphoto search for "1950s"

The reason for the difference in quality between stock imagery from Free Images and iStockphoto is quite simple. iStockphoto pays its artists. Therefore, the site attracts more submissions of higher quality. Purchasing images here is based on a credit system. Once you've created an account, you can purchase a pack of credits, which is sort of like buying tickets for a carnival. The price of each credit ranges from around $9 to $12. The more credits you buy, the cheaper they are. The standard "cost" for images on iStockPhoto ranges from two to 25 credits, depending on the size of image you need, and some images have a higher tariff. I know what you're thinking: $10 per credit times 25 credits is $250 per image. Typically on the Web, we only require one of the lower resolution image sizes, which cost between two and ten credits.

There are two things in particular to be aware of with credits:

- Buying credits doesn't solve all your problems. Like poker chips in a casino, they tend to disconnect you from the money you paid in. For instance, if you paid $22.50 for 11 credits on Site A and used four credits on an image, how much did you pay for that image? And how does that compare with the same image on Site B with a different credit system? There are no easy solutions to this, other than always keeping a strong sense of the cash value of a credit.

- Credits expire. Yes, that's right: if you don't consume your credits within a set period—usually a year from purchase date—they'll expire and become as worthless as old bananas in a fruit bowl. Unless stock providers are converting their revenues into bananas, there's no plausible, user-friendly reason to explain why a credit should have a shelf life. The takeaway? Don't be too quick to purchase a huge cache of discounted credits thinking you'll "use them eventually".

Another service that's similar to iStockphoto, but slightly less expensive, is Dreamstime[20]. While iStockphoto used to be my go-to resource, I've found that I can usually find what I'm looking for in Dreamstime's collection, which also features a growing number of free images. Depositphotos.com and Shutterstock.com are two other providers that, in my experience, offer a good balance of value and range.

 **Subscription Plans**

> Almost all stock providers offer a monthly/yearly subscription service. In the past, this often meant unlimited "all-you-can-eat" image downloads, but today it usually includes weekly or monthly cap limits. If your monthly image usage is consistent, subscriptions may be the most cost-effective option. However, I've found I might need 20 images one month and none the next, which nullifies any savings made with a subscription. Unless you're a big company, stick with the credit model.

## Rights-managed Images

A third level of stock photography service is known as **rights-managed**. This type of stock photography can be quite a bit pricier than the others, as you pay a fee based on the size of your business, the number of people who'll be exposed to the image, and the amount of time you'll need to use the image. Most of the larger stock providers—such as Corbis[21] and Getty Images[22]—have rights-managed options for their exclusive images. The photos in a rights-managed collection are usually of a professional quality.

---

[20] http://www.dreamstime.com/
[21] http://www.corbisimages.com/
[22] http://www.gettyimages.com/

Because the company in charge of the rights knows who's using the images and for how long, it's extremely unlikely that your client's competitor will have the exact same image on its home page that you've used for your client. With such a large pool of royalty-free images available, this may already seem improbable, but whether people notice it or not, this happens all the time.

TinEye[23] is a great tool for checking how widespread the use of a particular stock image is. This browser plugin touts itself as a reverse image search engine. You simply right-click on an image that you want to research and it searches for matches in its index of nearly two billion images. As you can see below, it will even find heavily modified versions of the original image. It's important to note here that, while there are many images of female customer service representatives with microphone headsets on stock photography sites, it's a horribly overused cliché. You should think twice before using this type of image, or any picture you can conceive involving business people standing around or shaking hands.

---

23. http://www.tineye.com/

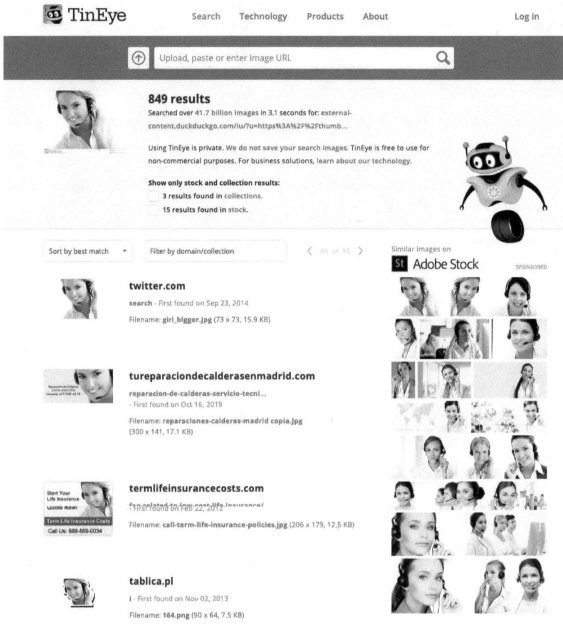

5-12. The TinEye search results for a popular Dreamstime image

While shelling out extra money for rights-managed photography may help your clients to avoid this type of scenario, there's no real guarantee of exclusivity. If you need to, the best option is to have photos taken professionally.

## Getting Professional Help

If you plan to hire a professional photographer to do your dirty work, be sure to find one who has experience with commercial photography and the type of shots you're looking for. That excellent photographer that captured your brother-in-law's tears at your cousin's wedding, for instance, may be great at portraiture and event shots, but might know nothing about architectural or product photography.

The best way to find a good commercial photographer is by word of mouth. If you know of other companies that have hired a professional photographer, ask them who they use on a regular basis, and what their experience is. If you don't have any references you can ask, try starting with a local professional association. If you're based in the United States, the American Photographic Artists website[24] is a great place to start. Many of the photographers listed in the APA database have biographies and portfolios that can give you a good idea of their capabilities.

To get an accurate handle on the costs, be very specific when writing a request for proposal. Be sure to include the details of each shot you need. State where you'd like to have the pictures taken if they're going to be done outside the photographer's studio, and be ready (with models, locations, wardrobes, and so on) to take all the pictures on the same day if possible. Most professional photographers charge by the day or half day. Daily rates can vary quite a bit, depending on the market and the photographer's experience, but they can range from just under one thousand to several thousand dollars. Another aspect to take into consideration is the photographer's copyright and usage guidelines. Many photographers will grant full ownership of the original photographs to your client upon payment. Some will require credit if the work is used in a commercial publication. A few photographers may require that they retain exclusive rights to the pictures they take, and they'll charge per use of the photos. You should try to negotiate full ownership and usage permissions whenever possible, but keep in mind that this type of contract may cost more.

If it's a professional illustrator you'd like to hire, another resource to look into is Hire an Illustrator[25]. This industry index hosts almost 500 artists, and makes it easy to find the person for the job by name, style, medium, or location.

24. http://www.apanational.com/
25. http://hireanillustrator.com/i/

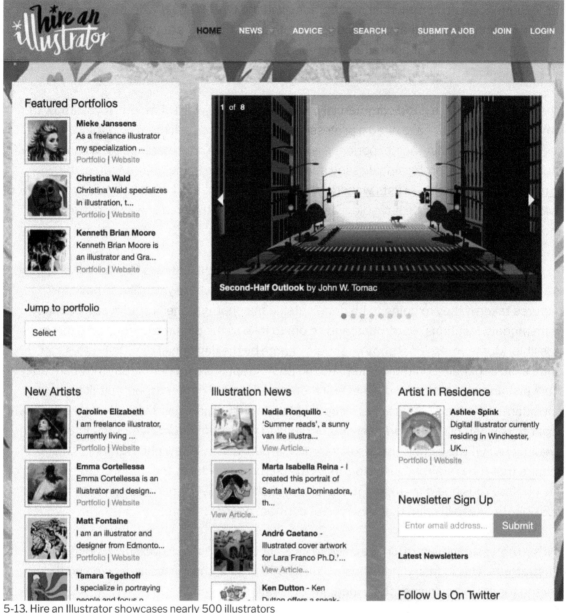

5-13. Hire an Illustrator showcases nearly 500 illustrators

As with hiring a photographer, though, the best way to find the right person for the job is often by word of mouth. If you live in or near a big city, chances are there are user groups or meetups for whatever branch of the web, tech, or design industry you're interested in. These are great places to find the talent you need to complete your next project, or even to hire for your team.

No matter what sources you use for your images—whether they're from a free stock website like Free Images, or whether a paid professional creates them—it's ultimately your clients who should have the final say. Even though it's likely you'll be choosing the images you feel best represent their company, sometimes your clients will disagree with your choices. Always be ready to adapt and make changes where necessary. As long as you're creating good work and acquiring your images from legitimate sources, your hard work should pay off, and the client will be impressed.

# How Not to Impress

So far, I've told you about a number of legitimate ways to obtain imagery for your projects. Now it's time to talk about how *not* to source imagery.

### Google Ganking

As a web designer, you may find inspiration by running a Google image search for topics you're building a website around. Let's say you're building a website for a bike shop. If the owner of the shop is yet to give you any images to work with, doing an image search for mountain biking, bike races, road bikes, and other related subjects can give you a better visual understanding of the topic, and an idea of the types of images you'll want to use on the site. Usually, this type of search will return some images that would work well in your design. You might even feel the urge to save some of these images to your computer, open them up in Photoshop, and crop, resize, and modify them a little to fit your needs. This is known as **Google Ganking**, and it's a serious problem in web design. Unless images on the Web are specifically marked as being free to use or available in the public domain, you can assume they're copyrighted, so you'll need permission to use them. You may think image owners will never notice you've ripped off their work, but you risk facing embarrassment when a cease-and-desist letter is sent to your client, or worse still, a lawsuit is filed against them.

### Hotlinking

If there's anything designers and website owners hate more than seeing their designs or images copied and reused, it's seeing them ripped off by a site that's linking directly to the original files. Usually, images for a website are placed on the same web server as the site, and are linked to like so:

```
<img src="/images/image.jpg" alt="Image Description" />
```

However, images can also be linked to from outside the website, using the full URL of the image:

```
<img src="http://www.somesite.com/images/image.jpg" alt="Image Description " />
```

Going back to my theoretical bike shop example, let's suppose I wanted to use a picture of a particular make and model of bike. Let's say I found an image of the right bike on the manufacturer's site and wanted to use it. Rather than requesting product images from the manufacturer, or even downloading the image and placing it on my client's web server, let's imagine I decide to link straight to the image on the bike manufacturer's website. This dubious practice is called **hotlinking**.

Copyright issues aside, hotlinking uses the bandwidth of the website on which the images are located. With most hosting accounts, bandwidth is limited, and extra bandwidth can be expensive. So as a real-world metaphor, hotlinking is a bit like using another person's cell phone minutes to make your call. Most web professionals know that hotlinking is a big no-no, so the usual hotlinking suspects are forum users, bloggers, and Tumblr users who don't know any better. So if you were unaware before, now you know better, too. Not to mention an additional problem with hotlinked images: the owner of the image could move or remove that image and replace it with something crude or embarrassing at any time.

## Clip Art

There are many websites that offer free, or very cheap, clip art and illustration packages. While these cheesy generic graphics may work for an internal company bulletin or do-it-yourself greeting card, they should be considered off limits for any professional project.

5-14. Clip art could make this happen to you!

You may think I'm being a little harsh with that statement, but take a moment to think about it. If you go to a five-star restaurant, would you expect to be served instant mashed potatoes from a box? Of course not! You'd expect fresh ingredients, cooked from scratch. As a designer, you have an obligation to cook something up for your client that's as original as it is astonishing. While the quality and "freshness" of stock photography can be questionable as well, there's nothing worse than seeing a good design blemished by stale, clichéd clip art. If your clients ask you to use clip art or a corny animated GIF on their site, you should push back a little. Just remember that if the client has come to you for the design, it's your job to provide feedback that'll make their site look good. However, you also have to remember that, ultimately, the client is always right. Sometimes a client will force a design decision, and you'll just have to go with it. I guess some people really like their instant potatoes.

# Image Presentation

Regardless of how good a job you've done choosing images for your design, there's another critical factor to consider: presentation. When you're formatting images for use on your site, their presentation will often depend on the constraints of the layout you've chosen. The image size, for instance, may depend on the size of the rectangle you have available in your grid. As the designer, it's up to you to determine how an image will be cropped, if an image will have any framing or borders, and what types of visual effects will be applied to the image, if any.

## Creative Cropping

One of the most profound impacts you can make on the presentation of an image comes from wisely choosing how much of it to use. This process is known as **cropping**, and is a fundamental image manipulation technique.

At its most basic level, cropping can be used to eliminate unnecessary or unsightly details from a picture. The picture below is one that I took while wandering around with my wife in downtown Charleston, South Carolina. It's an okay picture, but the people in the immediate foreground and the power lines that run down the shady right-hand side of the street are distracting.

5-15. An unedited photo of downtown Charleston

By cropping out some of the bottom and the right side of the photo, the edited image—shown below—feels less busy, more like a casual holiday shot. In the original photo, the perspective made the church steeple the focal point, but the image included too many other elements that competed for the viewer's attention. With the image cropped, the steeple is still the focal point, but the pair of shoppers jumps out as a secondary focus—due, in part, to the rule of thirds I talked about in Chapter 1. Even though the steeple is no longer in the center of the composition, the perspective lines that run along the top of the buildings, the edge of the road, and even the yellow line, point toward the steeple's base. Having this off-center element as the focal point of the image creates a more interesting composition, and helps to give the image a more intentional, balanced feel.

5-16. Charleston cropped

We can also crop images in unexpected ways to portray a sense of emotion, show an interesting perspective, or change the overall message of an image. Below, an image of a guitar player has been cropped tightly to show only the body of the guitar. This treatment highlights the sense of movement that's inherent in a musical performance, and provides a degree of anonymity that allows more people to connect with the image.

5-17. Tight cropping gives an image a sense of emotion and movement

 ## Size Matters

When cropping images tightly, like the guitar image above, it's important to be aware of the overall size of the image you're working with. You may want to crop to a very detailed area of the photo and then enlarge it, but if the image's resolution is too low, the cropped image will look pixelated (unless, of course, you're part of a TV crime drama, in which case you'll acquire magical powers to zoom in infinitely). Fortunately, images that are used on the Web can have much lower resolutions than those used in print, but always check the quality of your final image to make sure it's not grainy or blurry.

Images don't always have to be contained in boxes. Many of the fun and useful ways we can crop photos are more creative than just trimming off the sides. The photo below is one that I took from the banks of the Saluda River. I love this picture so much in its unedited form that I made it into a background image for my computer, but let's try to think outside the box.

5-18. The Saluda River

Unconventional cropping methods can come off as amateur if they're poorly executed, but if they're done well, they can be used to create some very striking graphics. Let's say I was designing a website for an outdoor center that rented kayaks for use on the Saluda River. In that case, I might use a technique like the one illustrated below.

5-19. The river image cropped around a kayaking shape

Here, I've used a vector image of a pair of kayakers as a mask around which to crop my original Saluda River picture. In image editing software, a mask is basically a window you can see the image through. When I laid the mask of the kayakers over the image of the river, I produced the top half of the image above. By flipping the mask vertically, and applying it to a blue-tinted duplicate of the original, I was able to create the appearance of a reflection.

Now that image might work for a kayak rental center website, but what if we were creating images for a website that promoted a regional visitor center? The center wouldn't want to limit the river as only being great for kayaking. It's also a great area for swimming, hiking, and fishing. By using the text "RIVER" as a mask below, I've made the image much more versatile, while establishing a fresh and creative look.

5-20. Using text as a mask to crop the Saluda River image

One final, non-rectangular approach to cropping involves removing part of an image from a scene. That part of the image we remove is known as a **knockout**. A knocked-out image can be featured without a background, placed onto another image, or even duplicated and rotated several times to make a flower. Okay, so maybe the last example of using a knockout as shown below is a bit far-fetched, but you have to admit that my banana flower looks fairly darn cool.

5-21. Knockout examples: bananas sans background, bananas in the sky, and a banana flower

As you can see, cropping provides endless possibilities for the production of unique images and design elements. The only limiting factors are your imagination and the ability to flesh out ideas in your photo editor.

## Image Adjustments

Although Photoshop occupies a less important role in my design workflow than it once did, it's still my tool of choice for correcting and perfecting photographs. In this section, we're going to look at a handful of useful Photoshop image adjustments, but don't worry if you don't have access to Adobe's Creative Cloud (which includes Photoshop). Each technique can be accomplished in Pixelmator[26], Affinity Photo[27] and even online tools like Pixlr[28].

When I'm taking personal pictures with my digital camera, I usually try to think a little about composition and lighting, but as I'm no real photography pro, my photos vary in quality. The not-so-great images often go straight to my personal photo gallery as records of places or events. If I'm taking a picture for a design project, though, these images always undergo some form of change before they're suitable for use in client work. At a minimum, the changes I'll make usually include cropping, and altering the brightness, contrast, and saturation of the photo.

The image below is an example of a photo straight from my digital camera. It's a picture of the amazing stonework around the entrance to the Biltmore Estate in Asheville, North Carolina, that I took during a visit last summer. It's an okay photograph, but it's definitely unfit for professional use. Even as a straight content image, it has competing focal points and feels unbalanced.

---

[26.] https://www.pixelmator.com
[27.] https://affinity.serif.com/en-gb/photo/
[28.] https://pixlr.com/

5-22. Another raw photo: the entrance of the Biltmore Estate

5-23. Initial cropping of Biltmore entrance carving

My first step is usually to crop the image to focus on the aspects I want to show. In this case, I plan to highlight the human figure to the right of the door. As a hypothetical scenario, let's say I want to use it for the feature image in a news article about the Biltmore Estate. I like the close-up of the sculpture in the image above, but I want to find a creative way to hide the eave over its head. One way I could achieve this would be to use an image box that cuts off that part, but shows the figure popping out of the top and left-hand sides.

To create this effect in Photoshop, I need two image layers: one that has the isolated stone figure, and another that has the background. I start out by duplicating my image several times, making sure to keep one completely unedited version in case I need to go back to step one. For the top layer, I carefully knock out the figure by zooming in and using the Polygonal Lasso tool to select the perimeter of the figure and cut off the excess. To create the background image, I use the Rounded Rectangle tool to create a mask of the area I want to show, then drag the mask onto my background box layer.

5-24. The Biltmore image double-cropped with two layers

The resulting image (above) looks quite good, but it could still use some adjustments. The first issue I have is that the grimy areas on the figure's shoulders and its shield are a bit unsightly. I'm not going to eliminate that completely, but I can take some steps to reduce the contrast in those areas. The tools for this job are the Dodge and Burn tools. The Dodge tool is a brush-like tool that actually lightens the area you click on, while the Burn tool darkens the area. By using these tools together, I can lighten the dark areas, and darken the light areas, to give the image more consistent shading and contrast.

Next, it's time to adjust the overall brightness and contrast of the two layers. Brightness and contrast are two controls that are provided by just about every image-editing tool. They can be accessed in the Photoshop menu via the **Image > Adjustments > Brightness/Contrast...**

option. The controls are shown below.

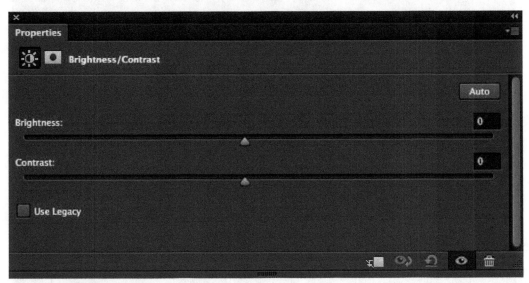

5-25. Photoshop's Brightness/Contrast controls

As we learned in Chapter 2, the brightness of an image actually refers to the overall amount of light or darkness in the image. The contrast of an image is the difference between the light and dark areas in the image. Kicking the brightness and contrast of the Biltmore figure up a few notches, and pushing the brightness and contrast of the background block down a bit, will help to give the composition a little more pop.

After I adjust the brightness and contrast, I move on to work on the hue and saturation. The Hue and Saturation controller shown below can be accessed via the **Image > Adjustments > Hue/Saturation...** menu option. The Hue control affects the overall color of the image. By moving the Hue slider up and down, you can shift the colors in the image so that it appears more blue, or red, or orange, and so on. The overall tone of this image is fine, so I don't really want to adjust its hue too much, but it's sometimes necessary to alter the hue if you want to change the overall color of an image.

The Saturation slider affects how saturated the colors appear within the image. If you turn the saturation off, you'll be left with a grayscale image, but if you turn it all the way up, all the colors will be brighter and more dramatic. I want to increase the saturation of the figure in the image, and reduce the saturation of the background. This will further highlight the contrast, and give the image the pop I was talking about before.

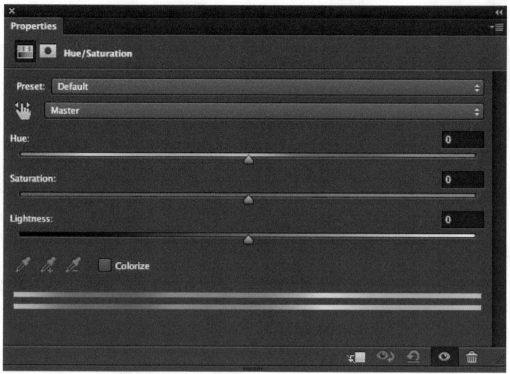

5-26. Photoshop Hue/Saturation Controls

5-27. The final image after Photoshop tweaking

Finally, the image is just about ready for posting! Notice how the figure above stands out from the background, and the shading is more even than before. These subtle details make a big difference to the overall effect of the image. To adjust a little more of that detail, I've applied an outline stroke around the background block by accessing **Layer > Layer Style > Stroke...** and giving the block an inside black stroke.

Besides making brightness, contrast, and saturation adjustments, another way to give an image a Photoshop facelift is by using filters.

## Filters

In earlier editions of this book, Photoshop filters were a worthy talking point. Back then, web browsers were much simpler creatures, and there was simply no way to re-style an image without editing its pixels in a photo editor like Photoshop, GIMP, or even MS Paint. That's not the case any more.

Today, we're at a point where permanently altering images for styling reasons should be your last resort. When we use CSS, we fully expect to be able to change layouts, color palettes, and typography choices from a single place without needing to re-author the content. Images are just another type of content and should be treated in the same way. Good content lasts; fashions come and go.

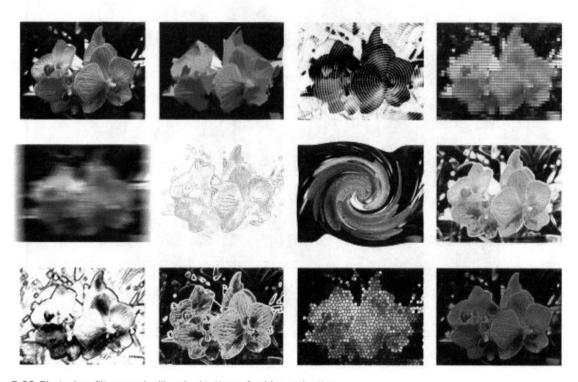

5-28. Photoshop filters can be like a bad tattoo: a fun idea at the time

Of course, that doesn't mean we should throw out Photoshop. As we saw earlier, raw photos nearly always need cropping, color correction, level adjustments and repairs to any issues that prevent them from presenting in their best natural state. But from there, always try to find "non-destructive", browser-based methods to style them. Here are a few ways to get you started.

## Styling Images with CSS Filters

CSS filters offer probably the simplest way to style images without permanently altering them. The table below shows the ten basic CSS filters we can use, which are all well supported by modern web browsers. The last in the list—the SVG filter—is the most complicated and powerful, so we'll cover that in the next section. The syntax for the remaining nine filters is relatively easy to follow.

| Filter | CSS | Value |
|---|---|---|
| **Blur** | `filter: blur(2px);` | px, em, mm, etc |
| **Brightness** | `filter: brightness(1.5);` | 0–10 |
| **Sepia** | `filter: sepia(.8);` | 0–1 |
| **Saturate** | `filter: saturate(3);` | 0–10 |
| **Invert** | `filter: invert(1);` | 0–1 |
| **Opacity** | `filter: opacity(.5);` | 0–1 |
| **Contrast** | `filter: contrast(1.6);` | 0–10 |
| **Drop shadow** | `filter: drop-shadow(3px 3px 5px rgba(0,0,0,0.9));` | (x-offset y-offset blur color) |
| **Hue rotate** | `filter: hue-rotate(90deg);` | 0deg–360deg |
| **SVG** | `filter: url("filters.svg#filter-id");` | *(hand coded)* |

No filter     filter: blur(2px);     filter: brightness(1.5);     filter: sepia(.8);     filter: saturate(3);

filter: invert(1);     filter: opacity(.5);     filter: contrast(1.6);     filter: drop-shadow(4px 4px 5px rgba(0,0,0,0.6));     filter: hue-rotate(90deg);

5-29. Examples of various CSS filters

Applying the filter to an image is straightforward. Create a new class (for example, I've called mine `.blur-me`) and add the filter property, filter type (such as `blur`), and value (`2px` for me):

```
<img class="blur-me" src="river.jpg" />
```

```
.blur-me {
  filter: blur(2px);
}
```

We can also combine CSS filters to create more complex effects:

```
.blur-me {
  filter: sepia(.5) contrast(1.2);
}
```

 **CSS Filters and Browser Performance**

> Be aware that applying lots of filters to lots of images can impact browser performance, so don't go too crazy.

Overall, you can see this gives us a lot of design scope that can be updated or removed with a few keystrokes. However, I'd argue the most powerful design magic comes when we begin to build our own filters from SVG and then call them via our CSS. That's a topic we could easily dedicate an entire book to, but let's look at a simple way to tap some of that power.

## Styling Images with SVG Filters

5-30. Five familiar-looking CSSgram filters

CSS Superhero <u>Una Kravets</u>[29] gives us a super-easy entry into using non-destructive SVG filter methods with her <u>CSSgram project</u>[30]. As it happens, SVG can reproduce most of the blend modes you find in Photoshop's layer panel (such as multiply, darken, color burn, and so on). Using blend modes to combine images with a colored gradient unlocks a ton of incredible effects, and CSS filters bring them through to our page. If you're an Instagram user, you'll probably recognize the names of some of the filters Una built using these SVG blend modes. Applying these pre-built filters to your own images is simple:

1. Download the <u>CSSgram</u>[31] Library.

2. Link that CSSgram library file within your project:

```
<link rel="stylesheet" href="where-your-css-lives/cssgram.min.css">
```

---

29. https://twitter.com/una
30. https://una.im/CSSgram/
31. https://raw.githubusercontent.com/una/CSSgram/master/source/css/cssgram.min.css

3    Wrap your image with a `<figure>` element and add the filter class:

```
<figure class="hudson">
    <img src="../img.png">
</figure>
```

Attaching this CSSgram file gives you access to 27 filters for less than 1KB. Of course, if you only needed one filter—which is probably a good idea—you could just copy that filter into your main CSS file. The only potential downside is that Internet Explorer support for SVG filters is patchy before 2019, so do some testing. I found about half the CSSgram filters work in 2018 Edge.

## File Formats and Resolutions

No matter which photo-editing program you use, to prepare images for the Web, you'll need to know a few basics about the standard image file formats and when each should be used. Currently, three image formats are widely supported by web browsers: JPEG, GIF, and PNG. Choosing the format that's right for your image is a matter of determining which will provide the smallest file size for the highest-quality image.

### JPEG

JPEG ( `.jpg` ) is an image compression format that was developed by the Joint Photographic Experts Group specifically to store photographic images. In most circumstances, JPEG will produce a smaller file size at 24-bit color than the equivalent PNG. This makes JPEGs great for any type of photography, or graphics with heavy textures or long gradients. Although there's no limit to the number of colors the JPEG format can display, it's a "lossy" format that can create visual artifacts depending on how much you compress the file. When saving a `.jpg` file, you'll have to carefully consider the amount of compression you apply. As you can see below, a highly compressed image might be great for page load speed, but if you go as far as I did with the right-most strawberry, it becomes blocky and blurry.

5-31. An image of a strawberry saved at increasingly higher levels of JPEG compression

## GIF

GIF (Graphics Interchange Format) is an 8-bit format that compresses files by limiting the number of colors in an image to a palette of (at most) 256 colors. It's like copying a photograph with a strict limit on the number of colored pencils you can use. Although the compression ratio of the GIF format is good, its 256 color limit is unsuited for most photographic images. Two nifty features of GIFs are that they display transparency (see below) and they support animation. In the late 1990s, UNISYS (the company behind the compression algorithm used in GIF images) tried to claim that GIF was a proprietary format, and charged companies royalties for any program that created GIF files. This—as well as the 256-color limitation of the format—led to the creation of the PNG format. Although the GIF format is still widely used on the Web, using PNG instead is strongly encouraged.

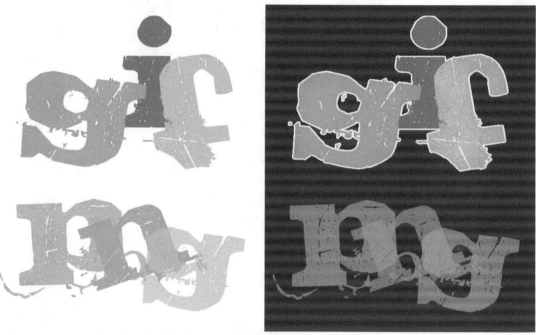

5-32. A transparent GIF and a 24-bit PNG, shown against different backgrounds

## PNG

The PNG (Portable Networks Graphics) format was developed by the W3C as an alternative to GIF. The lossless compression style of the PNG algorithm works similarly to that of GIF, in that files with fewer colors end up having the smallest file sizes. PNG images can be saved in either 8-bit (like GIF) or 24-bit (like JPEG) format. Both of these flavors of PNG support transparency, but transparency in 24-bit PNG images is implemented by means of an alpha channel that sits alongside the red, green, and blue channels. This means that each pixel in a PNG image can have up to 256 different levels of opacity. The effects of this difference are illustrated above: notice that you can still see the background image through the PNG image, while the GIF is either completely opaque or completely transparent. 8-bit transparency is like that of the GIF above: it's either on or off. Therefore, if you plan to put your transparent PNG image over a different background image or texture, you'll have to modify the image so that the opaque edges match the background. It's also worth noting that the 24-bit version of an image will be several times the size of its 8-bit cousin.

## Creative Image Treatments

Once you've inserted your JPEG, PNG, or GIF image into your web page, you may still find yourself a bit underwhelmed by its presentation. By default, images that are placed on a web page using an HTML `<img>` tag sit inline with the text that surrounds them. A hyperlinked image typically has a rather unattractive blue border. Not a very exciting default presentation, but that's what CSS is there for. What if you want to give an image a frame like one you might use to display a picture on your wall? What if you want an image to have a border around it that makes it look like a Polaroid picture? Perhaps you want it to have corner tabs like the ones you'd use to stick an image in a photo album. In each of these cases, you have two options: apply your desired effects directly to the photo using image-editing software, or use CSS background images and borders to style the image within your web page.

## Using Images to Enhance Images

Altering an image to add borders, edge effects, and transparency may seem like minimal hassle. It only takes a few minutes in Photoshop to give a photo the look you want. But problems can arise if you have to give every image on a website the same look. And what would happen if you had to add new images or change any of the existing pics? In either case, a task that would normally involve only a minor change to your HTML, plus a second or two to copy the new photo to the web server, might take half an hour or more. On top of that, the whole point of semantic markup is to separate style from content. An image in the content of a website is just that: a piece of content.

Although her site has sadly passed, graphic and web designer Wing Cheng had one of my favorite examples. With CSS turned off, Wing's portfolio simply looked like a page full of images, as shown below.

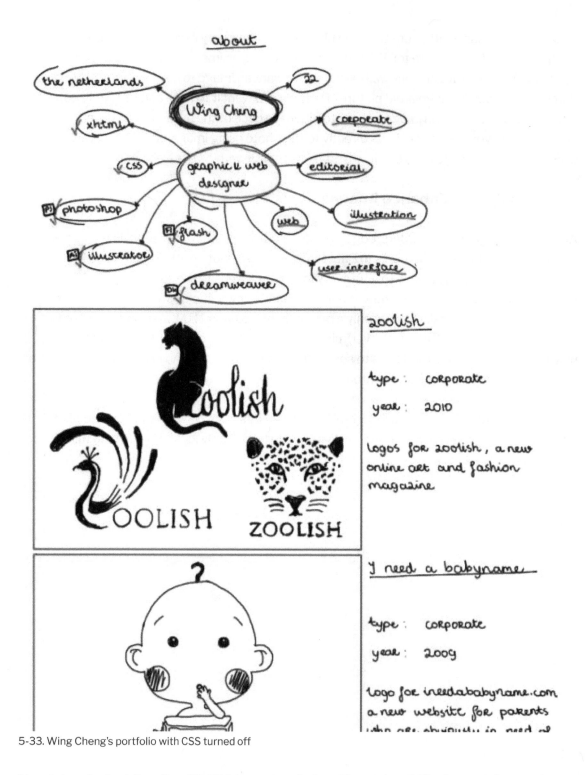

5-33. Wing Cheng's portfolio with CSS turned off

Now take a look at the site with CSS turned on, below. The style of Wing's portfolio was fun, whimsical, and creative. The paper pages angled in and out to give the appearance that it was a single 3D piece of paper that was accordion-folded. Each of the folds below the "about" page you see in the screenshot contained a single portfolio item. There were several items for each of the categories, and the site ended with a contact form and then the back cover of the leather sketchbook.

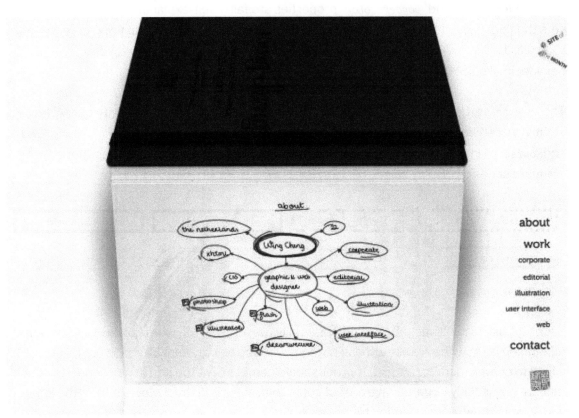

5-34. The creative portfolio of Wing Cheng

If Wing had incorporated the alternating page textures into the background of each portfolio item, the file size of each image would have been much larger, and the site would have taken too long to load. Instead, there were just two different paper textures—one angled in at the bottom and one angled out. These were applied as 24-bit PNG background images on the `div` elements that contained each portfolio item. If she wanted to add a new portfolio item, she only needed to shuffle the background images in the CSS, rather than having to recreate all the images for her entire portfolio.

In this example, the portfolio images were the content, and they were enhanced by the 3D paper backgrounds placed behind them.

## Using Pure CSS to Enhance Images

Applying a background or overlay is a great way to give your content images a unique and unified look. Of course, not all CSS-based image effects involve extra images. CSS borders provide myriad possible effects. As you may already know, the standard CSS2 borders have three properties—width, style, and color—which are controlled individually via the *border-width*, *border-style*, and *border-color* properties, and by the shorthand *border* property. The *border-width* and *border-color* properties are fairly self-explanatory. *border-width* sets the thickness of the border using either a CSS measurement (such as *1px* or *0.5em*) or a keyword (one of *thin*, *medium*, or *thick*). The *border-color* property takes a hexadecimal color value.

The *border-style* property is where the developers of CSS got their creativity on. We have eight visual styles to choose from: *dotted*, *dashed*, *solid*, *double*, *groove*, *ridge*, *inset*, and *outset*—in addition to the invisible values, *none* and *hidden*. You can see these standard styles on display below.

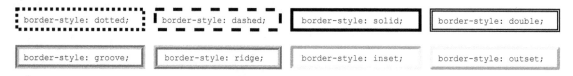

5-35. The eight built-in CSS border styles

Each style is clearly distinguished and potentially useful. I use the word "potentially" because, depending on how they're used, these borders can also be ugly. Just as good typography exists to complement text, a good border should complement the item it surrounds. Borders that are particularly large, or have a lot of color contrast, will distract viewers from the image you want to draw more attention to.

You can take full advantage of the ugly potential of these borders by specifying completely different borders for each side of a block. The ability to specify these values separately can be useful if you want a border on just one side of a block, or if you want to use different colors within the same border. But mixing different styles, colors, and thickness values around the same element or image usually only leads to trouble. As you can see from the scary monkey image below, this approach can produce some fairly horrific results (though I admit the toy itself doesn't help matters).

5-36. CSS can produce scary borders

Here's the CSS I used to create those scary borders:

```
img.uglybox {
  border-top: 20px groove #ff1100;
  border-right: 16px dotted #66ee33;
  border-bottom: 8px outset #00aaff;
  border-left: 12px double #ff00ff;
}
```

Thankfully, applying different CSS border properties to a single image doesn't have to be scary. The awesome power of borders can be used just as well for good as they can for evil. One graphic edge effect designers often apply to images to add dimension is a subtle drop shadow, inset or groove. I mentioned in Chapter 3 that CSS3 could be used to create drop shadows, but sometimes the effect you're going for is a little simpler and more subtle—like the one Claire Campbell employs on her site. In the figure below, you can see a real, working CSS digital clock. It was made by creatively manipulating CSS borders.

- 12/24
- **Color Scheme:**
- Green (Default)
- Red
- Glowing
- Tanfa - V.1
- Tanfa - V.2

5-37. Subtle groove on Claire's clock

## Breaking

Interestingly, if you're clever, there are even ways to break the sometimes tedious sharpness of CSS borders.

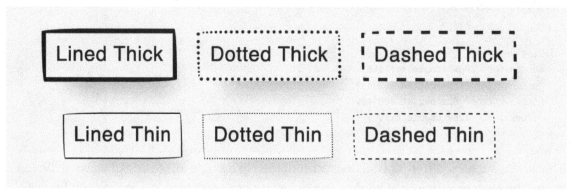

5-38. Hand-drawn CSS borders courtesy of Tiffany Rayside

Tiffany Rayside's <u>Imperfect Buttons</u>[32] use a fiendishly simple trick to create a range of what appear to be rough, hand-drawn CSS borders. There's no JavaScript, images, or tricky SVG hacks. What's the trick? There's a good chance you know that giving `border-radius` a single pixel value (or percentage) will apply that value to all four corners of an HTML element:

```
border-radius: 5px;
```

It's also fairly commonplace to provide four values that will be applied to each corner respectively—starting top left and going clockwise:

```
border-radius: 2px 6px 0px 13px;
```

---

[32] https://codepen.io/tmrDevelops/pen/VeRvKX

Tiffany has taken advantage of the less known and used ability to set a different radius for each *side* of a corner. Tiffany's eight border radius settings look like this:

```
border-radius: 255px 15px 225px 15px/15px 225px 15px 255px;
```

This is a great idea, and I've even seen examples using a handful of extra `:nth-of-type()` selectors to add a little more randomness to the mix.

It's an exciting time for web design and development. The example above represents just a tiny sliver of the new styling options in CSS3. For a full breakdown of the border properties, I recommend checking out Estelle Weyl's "Border Properties, Values, and Browser Support"[33] guide. The main goal with all these display effects is to bring more attention to the images in our content, whether it's done with creative overlays, simple border properties, or new CSS3 effects. The most important point to remember is that borders and effects should enhance the images they surround, not drown them out. Avoid adding effects that call more attention to themselves than to the image they're highlighting.

## The Project: Pulling the Design Together

So we have wireframes, a color palette, a pattern motif, and a solid typography system. It's time to stitch those elements together.

The basic typography grid that I established in Chapter 4 provides a system for sizing components and setting margins and padding. This makes life easier in three ways:

1   It helps keep visual consistency across the design.

2   It simplifies decision-making. If a top margin of two units isn't quite enough, it can really only be three.

3   Text rows will often (but not always) align with the top and bottom edges of adjacent images and other components.

---

33. http://www.standardista.com/css3/css3-border-properties

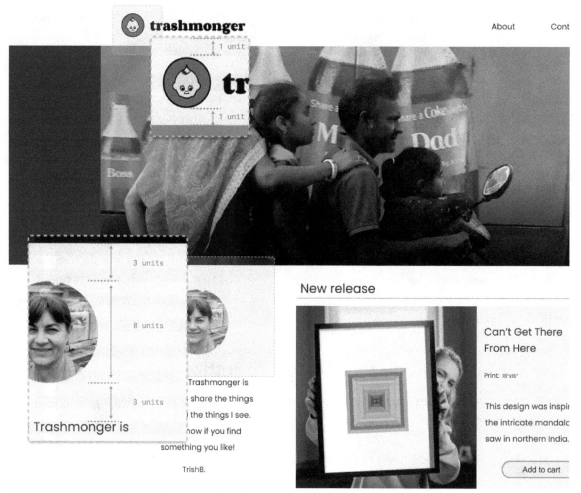

5-39. Heights and margins use the same grid system as your typography whenever practical

However, it's very likely that some page components simply won't fit perfectly into your grid. For instance, I have five square, parallel paintings and it just happens that squares of that width don't fit perfectly into my horizontal grid. And that's perfectly okay.

5-40. It's okay if not all page elements fit the grid perfectly

Sure, the text below shifts up a little, but the overall sense of harmony and balance isn't broken by a handful of exceptions. The grid advises; it doesn't demand.

**Importing Existing HTML or CSS into Figma**

While most design tools offer HTML/CSS export, often it can be useful to be able to *import* existing HTML/CSS into your design (such as the code we got from Gridlover). In my experience, Figma seems to offer the best HTML import options.

5-41. The HTML to Figma Plugin

Builder.io have developed an excellent, free Figma plugin called "<u>HTML to Figma</u>",[34] which converts any URL into a Figma file. This can be paired with a <u>Chrome Extension</u>[35] that even allows you to import HTML from your local system. I've had impressive results with this plugin. PNGs and JPEGs are converted to blank rectangles, but most typography, linework and color is faithfully rendered ready to work with.

Note that there's also an <u>equivalent HTML-to-Sketch</u>[36] project on GitHub, but I've had less success with it in my limited testing.

## Pulling in the Pattern Motif

It's time to integrate our pattern. I'm going to use it quite boldly at the edges of the hero section, as this will be cropped off on smaller screens. Further down, I'm going to use it as a patterned border ribbon on the dark panel sections. It's providing a lot of visual bang for buck.

---

[34] https://www.figma.com/community/plugin/747985167520967365/HTML-To-Figma

[35] https://chrome.google.com/webstore/detail/html-to-figma/efjcmgblfpkhbjpkpopkgeomfkokpaim

[36] https://github.com/KimDal-hyeong/html-to-sketch-electron

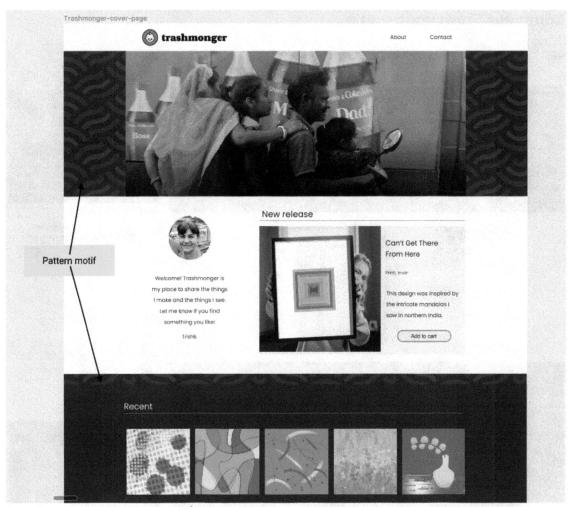

Pattern motif

5-42. The pattern motif adds some depth and detail

## Complete: Trashmonger v1.0

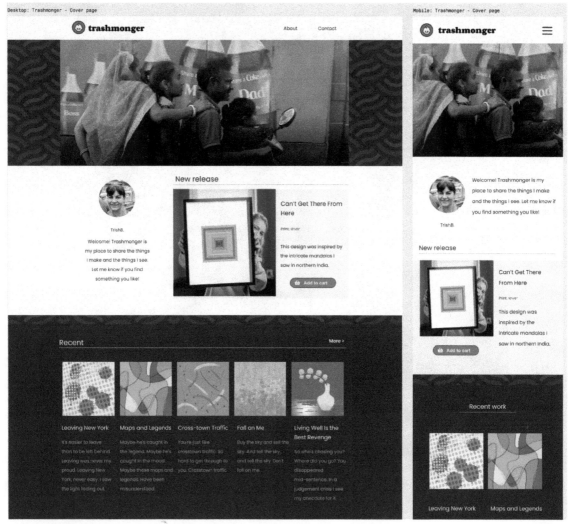

5-43. The final working design shown in desktop and mobile views

Here's the final design—although, in my experience, final designs are never *that* final. The five-column layout was fun to work with, even if it did make the mobile design more complicated. Overall, it's a relatively easy layout to build, it should load quickly, and it should be a good vehicle for showing off the artwork. That's a good starting place.

## Onward and Upward

One of the most exciting aspects about designing for the Web is the sense of community and interaction that exists among web professionals. Whether it's on blog comments, Twitter, Dribbble[37], SitePoint Community[38] or even local tech meetups, there are always talented people who are willing to share their opinions, techniques, and expertise. The design community truly is an invaluable resource—but it can also become an unnecessary crutch. I'm always looking for new sources of inspiration, and because there are so many authoritative designers out there who offer their ideas and portfolios online, it would be easy for me to find all the inspiration I need from web design alone. In and of itself, that isn't so bad, but if every web designer is getting their ideas from other web designers, eventually we'll all end up with the same designs.

While the design principles and guidelines we've discussed throughout this book can help you make aesthetically pleasing and practical design decisions, they're no substitute for character and originality. The most important resources you can bring to the design table are your own personality, experiences, and interests. These three resources should form the foundations of your design work. If every designer spent less time trying to emulate the latest design trends and more time defining their own style, the Web would be a much more interesting place. While I'd love to be able to tell you how to define your own style, I'm continually trying to learn what this is for myself. I wish you the best of luck in your future design endeavors, and hope you've found this book to be both helpful and encouraging as you kick off a career—or hobby—in web design.

37. http://dribbble.com/
38. https://www.sitepoint.com/community/